DOES THIS TASTE FUNNY?

Stephen Colbert &
Evie McGee Colbert

DOES THIS TASTE FUNNY?

Recipes Our Family Loves

Photography by
ERIC WOLFINGER

CELADON
BOOKS
NEW YORK

ALSO BY STEPHEN COLBERT

I AM AMERICA (And So Can You!)

*AMERICA AGAIN: Re-Becoming
the Greatness We Never Weren't*

The Library of Congress Cataloging-in-Publication Data
Names: Colbert, Stephen, 1964– author. |
Colbert, Evelyn McGee, author. |
Wolfinger, Eric, photographer.
Title: Does this taste funny? : recipes our family loves /
Stephen Colbert & Evelyn McGee Colbert ;
photography by Eric Wolfinger. Description: First edition.
| New York, NY : Celadon Books, 2024. | Includes index.
Identifiers: LCCN 2024004862 |
ISBN 9781250859990 (hardcover) |
ISBN 9781250380715 (ebook) |
Subjects: LCSH: Cooking, American—Southern style. |
Cooking—South Carolina. | LCGFT: Cookbooks.
Classification: LCC TX715.2.S68 C664 2024 |
DDC 641.5975—dc23/eng/20240212
LC record available at https://lccn.loc.gov/2024004862

Our books may be purchased in bulk for promotional,
educational, or business use. Please contact your
local bookseller or the Macmillan Corporate and Premium
Sales Department at 1-800-221-7945, extension 5442, or
by email at MacmillanSpecialMarkets@macmillan.com.

Book design by Toni Tajima
Food styling by Alison Attenborough
Prop styling by Lisa Jean Walsh and Alma Espinola
Wardrobe styling by Lisa Jean Walsh

First Edition: 2024

10 9 8 7 6 5 4 3 2 1

Dedication

The term "Southern Hostess" is overused, but Evie's mother, Patti McGee, was the real thing.

Patti McGee, May 1991

If the doorbell rang unexpectedly, she would stop whatever she was doing and welcome in whoever it was for a cool glass of iced tea or something stronger, depending on the time of day. She always had a tin filled with a fresh batch of her cheese biscuits at the ready, but it was really her smile that made guests feel right at home.

When she learned we were writing this book, she set out to help in any way that she could. We pulled out her dog-eared cookbooks to remember how she had refined classic Southern recipes over the years. We crawled through the attic to find her mother-in-law's recipe box that we had feared was lost for good. She tasted and critiqued everything we made for her and allowed us to publish some of her recipes that she had never shared before.

All this time she was fighting cancer, and even when she was in the hospital, we would sit together and talk about food and cookbooks and how we could make ours special.

Though she didn't live to see this book published, she is a part of every page. With love and admiration, we dedicate this book to her.

CONTENTS

Introduction
1

PARTY FOOD
9

SOUPS
57

POULTRY
83

MEAT
115

SEAFOOD
145

VEGETABLES, SIDES, AND ONE OTHER THING
179

DESSERTS
221

BREAKFAST
261

DRINKS
295

Thank-Yous
317

Index
318

INTRODUCTION

Hi. I'm **STEPHEN COLBERT.**   *Hello. I'm* **EVIE COLBERT.**

STEPHEN • *Not McGee?*

EVIE • *Not today.*

STEPHEN • *Okey-doke. So, darling, we have never written a cookbook before. How did this happen?*

EVIE • *Because of Covid, I think.*

STEPHEN • *Folks, that's what we in The Business call a "grabber." I'm intrigued. Go on.*

EVIE • *Well, it was during lockdown, so we were all stuck together, and we couldn't go out to eat, so we cooked. We had all three kids back under our roof again, and for the first time in a long time, we had dinner together each night as a family. We were in Charleston doing* The Late Show *from our house, and since the five of us had to be the cast and crew (on top of having our own jobs, classes, and other responsibilities), there was a lot of collective stress, and cooking together became a major source of entertainment.*

STEPHEN • *I loved that the whole family worked on the show.*

EVIE • *It was fun.*

1

STEPHEN • *I had always been nervous about working with you. I was afraid that working together wouldn't be fun for you, because I am used to being the boss.*

EVIE • *Especially in the kitchen . . .*

STEPHEN • *Oh, here it comes . . .*

EVIE • *That's why I think it's ironic that we're doing a cookbook together, because . . .*

STEPHEN • *Oh, no. Are you gonna tell the spoon story?*

EVIE • *No, not the spoon story. But very early on in our marriage, I had visions of us sipping wine and chopping basil together while listening to, I don't know . . .*

STEPHEN • *Chet Baker.*

EVIE • *Sure. And those dreams were dashed the first time you corrected the way I chopped basil or something.*

STEPHEN • *I have never corrected the way you chop basil or something. OK. Clearly, writing a cookbook was a huge mistake. You're gonna tell the spoon story.*

EVIE • *No, because I indict myself in the spoon story. Here's the thing: We're different in the kitchen. You're a curious and adventurous cook, because you're an improviser, and I'm a rule follower. I like steps.*

STEPHEN • *Which is why you're a better baker than I am.*

EVIE • *You love the creative act of cooking.*

STEPHEN • *I like how one set of ingredients becomes another thing entirely. It's* like magic—a transformation of raw materials into intentional pleasure.

EVIE • *And I love the comforting aspect of cooking—nourishing, supporting, and showing love to someone else. Left alone, I would never cook a meal.*

STEPHEN • *And left alone I would cook my most ambitious meal.*

EVIE • *I like making food for other people.*

STEPHEN • *You're a nice person. I'm terrible.*

EVIE • *You're bossy, I'm compliant.*

STEPHEN • *You're a saint.*

EVIE • *I'm insecure.*

STEPHEN • *I'm overconfident.*

EVIE • *You say "recipe."*

STEPHEN • *You say "receipt."*

EVIE • *At some point we should probably address the "recipe/receipt" issue.*

STEPHEN • *Yes. The people deserve an explanation. I say "recipe" because I live in America in the twenty-first century. Why, throughout this book, do you say "receipt"?*

EVIE • *Well, I suppose because my mom always said "receipt." She was a young wife in 1960. She had come to the Big City of Charleston from little Marion, South Carolina, and I think she learned most of her cooking from* The Charleston Receipts Cookbook. *Saying "receipts" was a way of indicating that she knew the traditional recipes.*

STEPHEN • *I love archaic words, so I love "receipt." Did you know that "receipt" comes from the days when you wouldn't* take a cookbook out of your library to the kitchen, because books were precious, and it might get ruined in there, what with the fire and grease and whatnot. Instead, you copied down a "receipt" of the instructions and took that piece of paper to the kitchen. So I like that you say "receipt."

EVIE • *It might also be that I'm just a bad speller.*

STEPHEN • *A strong possibility. We talk a lot about the Lowcountry and Lowcountry cooking. We should probably explain what that is.*

EVIE • *Well, the Lowcountry is where we grew up—coastal South Carolina. Lowcountry cooking is classic Southern fare, but it's heavy on seafood and rice. Really, though, you can't talk about Lowcountry cooking without talking about the influence of the Gullah Geechee culture of the Sea Islands.*

STEPHEN • *So much of what we think of as "local" ingredients are actually staples of West African cooking: red rice, okra, black-eyed peas, collards, watermelon, benne seeds, boiled peanuts. And during the five months we did the show from South Carolina, we not only rediscovered those essential ingredients that we grew up with, we were with the family and friends who had originally taught us those recipes—many of whom appear throughout this book.*

EVIE • *Though these aren't just Southern receipts. These are our favorite dishes wherever they come from. Some we invented, and some we got from friends and family.*

STEPHEN • *Yes, there are many guest appearances. But this whole thing started with you in a headset, laughing at my jokes, while I did the show from our spare bedroom.*

EVIE • *We were cooking together, living together, working together, and all the while quite literally inviting the audience into our home. Surprisingly, we didn't kill each other.*

STEPHEN • *That was a positive outcome. We actually enjoyed it, so we wanted to find another way to work together and share a little more of our lives, and this is it. Hopefully, reading this book and cooking these recipes will feel like hanging out with us in the kitchen.*

EVIE • *Welcome to our home. We basically live in the kitchen anyway.*

STEPHEN • *So, to recap: this book exists because we were forced to do the show from home during Covid, and we worked well together, which is ironic, because I'm awful.*

EVIE • *You're not awful. You are bossy. As we all know from the spoon story.*

STEPHEN • *And I'm afraid we're out of time . . .*

PATTI McGEE'S
CHEESE BISCUITS
12

CRABMEAT QUICHE
FOR COCKTAIL HOUR
15

SULLIVAN'S ISLAND
SHRIMP PASTE
19

PICKLED SHRIMP
23

AUGGIE'S FENNEL-
BOURBON CANDIED
HOT PEPPERS
27

HOT
CRABMEAT DIP
30

WARM
ARTICHOKE DIP
33

CLAUS BOILS
SOME PEANUTS
34

CAYENNE
PEPPER–PIMENTO
CHEESE SPREAD
36

COWBOY CAVIAR
39

GREEN GODDESS DIP
40

BACON-WRAPPED
DATES STUFFED WITH
MARCONA ALMONDS
43

DAD'S
DEVILED EGGS
44

SIVVY BEAN
HUMMUS
47

COURGETTE
"MADELEINES"
48

CHICKPEA FRIES
(PANELLE)
52

PARTY
FOOD

Stephen and I love a good party, and making the food that we will serve our friends just adds to the anticipation. As I pull the bacon-wrapped dates from the oven, I can almost taste the first drink. You'll notice some of the receipts in this chapter are quite filling, and that's no accident. Party food is happy food, and we like to fill up on happy whenever we can.

I remember, many times, being told by my parents on the way out the door to a cocktail party, "Be sure to eat a lot of whatever they're passing, because that's your dinner." Stephen and I have adopted that same philosophy with our kids whenever possible. Why bother serving a balanced meal when you can just allow your children to belly up to the cheese dip? That's why we called this chapter Party Food instead of Appetizers. "Appetizers" implies something to follow. In our house, this is often the only course.

All of the receipts in this chapter are excellent for a gala or a get-together of any kind, but, most importantly, they are a delicious invitation to slow down and relax with your family and friends. • **EVIE**

Patti McGee's
CHEESE BISCUITS

EVIE • *My mother, Patti McGee, made these cheese biscuits for years and years. She became quite famous among her friends for having mastered the perfect receipt for this classic Southern savory biscuit. Every Christmas Eve when we were young, my sister and I would hop in the car with my father and deliver boxes of Mom's cheese biscuits to nearly everyone we knew, it seemed. Even toward the end of her life, when she was not well, Mom did not stop making them. Instead, she set up a production line and oversaw things with an eagle eye. My father was given the job of head cheese grater, which he accepted eagerly. Mom would sift the flour and melt the cheese and Mom's helper, Mary Branton, would roll the biscuits out onto the cookie sheets. The moment they went into the oven, Dad's job was to turn the kitchen timer to 15 minutes. They were a marvel of efficiency. Christmas of 2021, they made over twenty batches! After Mom died in November of 2022, my sister and I stepped in and shared her role. Together with Dad and Mary's help, we made enough batches to deliver to all of Mom's friends around town. It is an honor to share this receipt with you, because Mom held it as a closely guarded family secret. But she was so excited about our cookbook that she absolutely wanted her cheese biscuits to be included.*

STEPHEN • *These biscuits will always be the holidays for me. A bourbon and a cheese biscuit is the taste of the season, and my favorite way to start any party. They will always remind me of Patti's enormous heart and welcoming smile.*

Stephen says
Serve with a bourbon and soda.

Makes about 50 biscuits

8 tablespoons (1 stick) margarine (see Note)

8 tablespoons (1 stick) salted butter (see Note)

½ pound extra sharp cheddar cheese (see Note)

2 cups sifted self-rising flour, or as needed

Several dashes of cayenne pepper

1 egg white

About 50 nice pecan halves

~~~~~~~~~~~~~~~~~~~~~~~~~~~~

NOTE

• Mom found that this recipe was most successful with Land O'Lakes butter and Land O'Lakes margarine (Imperial margarine will also do) and Cracker Barrel extra sharp cheddar cheese.

Pour 2 inches of water into the bottom of a double boiler. If you don't have a double boiler, use a heavy 3- to 4-quart saucepan.

Melt the margarine and butter in the top of the double boiler; the water in the bottom of the double boiler shouldn't be too hot, definitely not boiling. Or, if using a saucepan, melt the margarine and butter over very low heat. When they are completely melted, remove the top of the double boiler (or the saucepan) from the heat. Add the cheese slowly, stirring until it is combined with the margarine and butter. Add the sifted flour and as many dashes of cayenne as you like into the cheese all at once and stir until all the flour is mixed in. If the dough seems too soft, add a little more flour. Set the dough aside until cool enough to handle, about 20 minutes. You can also refrigerate the dough for up to several hours, but be sure to bring the dough to room temperature for about 20 minutes before rolling it out.

While the dough is cooling, heat the oven to 325°F with one rack in the upper third position and one in the lower third. Or, if you'd rather just roll and bake one sheet of biscuits at a time, you'll only need one rack in the center position.

Whip the egg white in a small bowl with a fork until foamy.

Roll the dough into walnut-sized balls, setting them about 2 inches apart on an ungreased baking sheet as you go. If the dough seems a little crumbly when you start to roll it into balls, just give it a second; the warmth from your hands will soften it up and make for smooth rolling.

One at a time, dip a pecan in the egg white and press it lightly onto the top of a dough ball.

Bake until the biscuits are puffy and lightly browned, about 15 to 20 minutes. (You'll know they're done when the kitchen smells wonderful!)

Cool the biscuits on the pans for 5 minutes, then move them to a cooling rack to cool completely. Cheese biscuits can be stored in an airtight container at room temperature for up to 4 days.

CRABMEAT QUICHE
for Cocktail Hour

EVIE • *In 1977, Gian Carlo Menotti created the Spoleto Festival USA in Charleston, South Carolina, as a companion to the Festival dei Due Mondi in Spoleto, Italy. My family lived next door to the Dock Street Theater at the time, and Maestro Menotti asked my mother if she would host occasional parties at our house for the musicians who were performing next door. As was her way, Mom replied instantly: "I would be delighted to." And so, for the next twenty years, every day during the two-week festival, my parents opened their home to the visiting chamber musicians and their friends. My sister and I were eager helpers. We passed cheese biscuits and poured lemonade for days and loved every minute of it.*

This quiche has plenty of crab and Swiss cheese, all wrapped in a flaky crust. It was one of the receipts Mom served at her parties. She made them as bite-sized quiches, and they were wildly popular. The crabmeat makes it a bit expensive for cocktail food, but these are so filling that you can make a meal out of them.

STEPHEN • *I'll just jump in here to say that Evie and I met at the Spoleto Festival in May of 1990, even though I had lived one street away from her since 1977. We ran with different crowds, because one of us is a year older, and I'm not supposed to say who. Evie says it's good that we waited so long to meet, because she may not have liked the younger me. First of all, I have always been delightful. Second, Patti's Spoleto parties sound fun, I'm sorry I missed them, and I blame Evie's unwillingness to meet me.*

continued ⟶

All-Purpose Food Processor
Pie Pastry (page 232)

1 cup crabmeat, preferably
lump, picked over for bits
of shell

1 cup coarsely grated Swiss
cheese (3 to 4 ounces)

3 green onions, trimmed and
thinly sliced

1½ cups light cream or half-
and-half

3 large eggs

1 tablespoon dry or cream
sherry

1½ teaspoons salt

½ teaspoon nutmeg,
preferably freshly grated

¼ teaspoon freshly ground
pepper

You'll need pie weights or
uncooked rice or beans and
a 13 × 9 × 1-inch baking pan
(aka "quarter sheet pan").

Make the pastry shell: Pat the full recipe of pastry into a rectangle (instead of a circle) somewhere close to 4 × 6 inches and chill for at least 1 hour, and up to 1 day.

Roll the chilled pastry into a 16 × 12-inch rectangle, rolling it only away from you and giving it a quarter-turn after each pass with the rolling pin. Starting at one of the short ends, roll the pastry up around the rolling pin, then unroll it into a 13 × 9 × 1-inch baking pan, centering it evenly. Gently tuck the pastry into the corners of the pan. Trim the dough as necessary so it overhangs by ½ inch all around the pan. Tuck the overhanging dough inside the pan so there is a double thickness of pastry at the top of the shell. Crimp the top edges with a fork or your fingers, or score lightly with a paring knife. Refrigerate the shell for at least an hour, and up to 3 hours.

Heat the oven to 350°F with a rack in the lower position.

After the shell has rested, line it with a sheet of aluminum foil or parchment paper. (Crumpling up and then unfolding the parchment will make it easier to mold it to the shape of the pastry shell.) Fill the lined shell with pie weights, uncooked rice, or dried beans to weigh it down.

Bake the shell for 20 minutes. Remove the liner and weights and poke the bottom of the shell all over with a fork. Return the shell to the oven and bake until the edges are very lightly browned, about 15 minutes. Move to a cooling rack and let cool to room temperature. The shell can be baked up to several hours in advance and kept at room temperature.

When the shell is completely cooled and you're ready to make the quiche, heat the oven to 425°F with a rack in the lowest position.

Drain the crabmeat, if necessary. Scatter the crab, cheese, and half the green onions over the bottom of the shell so they come all the way to the sides and into the corners. Whisk the cream, eggs, sherry, salt, nutmeg, and pepper together in a medium bowl until well blended.

Pull out the oven rack, put the pan on the rack, and carefully pour in the custard mix. Scatter the remaining green onions over the top. Gently slide the rack back in. Immediately reduce the oven temperature to 350°F and bake until a knife inserted in the center of the quiche comes out clean, 25 to 30 minutes. Serve warm, cut into 1 × 2-inch rectangles, or smaller for bite size.

Sullivan's Island
SHRIMP PASTE

STEPHEN • *We are well aware how offputting the word "paste" is. If it helps, think of this as a shrimp pâté. There are many versions of this, and variations are easy to try, but we have included the simplest and, we think, the best. Try varying the amounts of each ingredient if you like. It's hard to hurt this recipe.*

This shrimp paste is surprisingly versatile. It makes a tasty spread at cocktail hour, exceptional finger sandwiches, served on tomato slices, or accompanying a nice fluffy scrambled egg. I have a pound of it in my fridge right now, and I'm fighting the urge to stop this typing and eat it all. With a fork. Standing at the open refrigerator door.

EVIE • *Shrimp paste is one of those things Charlestonians eat from an early age. Some kids have Brie cheese or smoked salmon and feel grown up; for us, it was shrimp paste. It was served at every party we went to, and I mean every party! When Stephen and I first met, he told me he could make his own shrimp paste. This was very impressive to me. I didn't really cook anything in my twenties. Luckily this recipe is NOT what he made me all those years ago. It is much better!*

STEPHEN • *This is a tough way to find out my old shrimp paste was awful. And yet, you still married me.*

Stephen says

Shrimp paste is good. It will be better tomorrow. Is the party today? Try making this yesterday.

Makes about 2 cups

Shrimp boil seasoning, such as Old Bay

1 pound medium shrimp (preferably fresh local shrimp)

Half a medium onion, finely diced

⅓ cup mayonnaise

2 to 3 dashes Tabasco or other hot sauce

Salt and freshly ground white pepper (if you have it—if not, black pepper will do fine)

Bring a good amount of water to boil in a large pot. While it is heating, add a generous amount (6 to 8 tablespoons) of the boil seasoning to the water and set a large bowl of half ice/half water near the sink. When the water is at a rolling boil, add the shrimp and cook for 3 minutes . . . no more! Drain in a colander and then immediately place them in the ice bath. (This will "shock" them and keep them from overcooking and turning tough.)

When the shrimp have cooled, drain them, then peel and devein them (see the sidebar). Finely dice the shrimp, putting them in a medium bowl. Add the onion, then add the mayonnaise, mixing them thoroughly with the shrimp. Hit the mixture with a few dashes of Tabasco and salt and pepper to taste. Refrigerate until ready to serve.

PEELING AND DEVEINING SHRIMP

So many shrimp are sold already peeled and deveined that peeling them at home may have become a lost art. But look for shrimp in the shell—they'll make for tastier cooked shrimp. Whether you're peeling shrimp before or after cooking, the technique is pretty much the same: Remove the heads if necessary. Grab the tail of each shrimp and pinch/pull it away from the shrimp, leaving the tail meat intact. Then slip your finger under the shell at the spot where the legs meet the flesh and simply take the "jacket" off the shrimp. To devein them, run a paring knife gently along the "spine" of each shrimp and pull out the dark line. (Paper towels come in handy here for wiping.)

STEPHEN SHARES HIS SHRIMPY THOUGHTS *(bonus rant included)*

While the Lowcountry of South Carolina has every type of seafood you could want—even lobster, if you know where to look off the coast—it's best known for the local shrimp. We can't impress this upon you forcefully enough—whenever possible, get fresh local shrimp. The difference between local shrimp and "shrimp" is like the difference between ice cream and ice. One of them is paradise; one is flavorless and hard.

We both learned how to catch our own shrimp out of the creek. With drop net, cast net, or seine, most of the year you'll have pretty good luck. One of my most vivid childhood memories of my father is shrimping with him off a pier in Charleston Harbor. We were using a drop net and hadn't had much luck all day, but then it began to rain. It was warm summer rain, big fat drops without a breath of wind, just falling like pebbles into the dark water off James Island, where we lived. For whatever reason, in that dead rain, the water came alive with shrimp, and suddenly we were pulling up net after net loaded with the pearl-gray beauties, flipping and popping about as we dumped them into our Coleman cooler. We stood there laughing in the downpour, amazed at our luck. When the cooler was full, my dad told me to drain the water so we could fit in more shrimp. At ten years old, I didn't know there was a drain plug, so naturally, I tipped the cooler to let the water out. I lost control of it

and spilled all the shrimp back into the harbor. My father looked at the water, at the empty cooler, and then at me. I don't remember him being angry. I don't remember what he said at all, but I do know that I don't know if I have always been so patient with my own children. All I remember was both of us worrying that no one would believe how many shrimp we had caught.

bonus rant!

A word on how shrimp is served. If you are having it "peel and eat" style, any way you want to serve it is fine with me: hot, cold, head on, head off, shell on, shell off. But!

If the shrimp has been prepared in a sauce of any kind, I have some thoughts: Many's the time that I have been in a restaurant—a good restaurant at that—and ordered, say, a shrimp pasta in a sauce, and it arrives at my table with the tails still on the shrimp. What are they thinking? Am I expected to eat the tails? They're pointy and crunchy. They're like toenail clippings in marinara. So, what am I supposed to do? Take off my jacket, roll up my sleeves, and use my fingers to remove the tails? Will the restaurant provide me a wet bar towel to clean my hands? Why not just serve a steak with the hoof still on? Why do they do it? Do they think it looks "fancy"? Are they lazy? Why do they expect me to cut off the tails? Are they going to discount my check for the labor and lost tail meat? When I cut them off, am I expected to lay them on the rim of the bowl like miniature hunting trophies? Do I seem angry about this? Good, because I am.

If this book can achieve only one thing, I hope it is to end the travesty of the decorative shrimp tail.

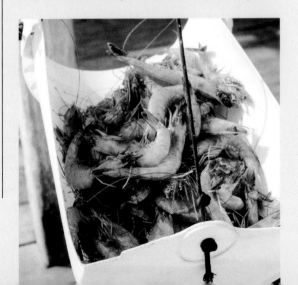

Pickled
SHRIMP

EVIE • *We eat a lot of shrimp. Growing up in Charleston, there were three food groups: shrimp, barbeque, and everything else. This is my mother's receipt, which she basically made up. When we started working on this book, Mom and I had fun trying to remember exactly what she put into her pickled shrimp. We had to make it several times just to double-check we had it right. I recommend serving this on a hot summer's day with an ice-cold glass of rosé. There is nothing better!*

STEPHEN • *"There is nothing better!" Fact check: Evie is a Pinot Grigio girl all the way. I think she chose rosé here because of how pretty it looks in the photo on the facing page. I apologize for her dishonesty. I've never known her to lie before.*

This is my mother-in-law's recipe, but when I went to test it, I didn't have white vinegar, so I used rice vinegar. I liked it. It's a little sweet, but that pairs well with the rosé that I, for one, will be drinking.

continued ⟶

Makes about 24 shrimp

2 bay leaves

1 pound (21–25 count) shrimp, preferably in the shell

¾ cup vegetable oil

½ cup white vinegar (or rice vinegar)

1½ teaspoons sugar, or to taste

1 teaspoon celery salt

¾ teaspoon salt, or to taste

2 tablespoons drained capers

Half a large bell pepper (red is nice), cored, seeded, and thinly sliced

1 medium yellow onion, thinly sliced

1 tablespoon Auggie's Fennel-Bourbon Candied Hot Peppers (page 27), finely chopped, or 1 teaspoon sugar plus ½ teaspoon red pepper flakes

Bring 5 cups water and one of the bay leaves to a boil in a medium saucepan. Set a large bowl of half ice/half water near the sink. When the water comes to a boil, lower the heat to a simmer and gently slide in the shrimp. Cook until they are pink and any translucence is gone, 2 to 3 minutes. Use a slotted spoon to move the shrimp to the ice bath, then drain once cooled.

Whisk the oil, vinegar, sugar, celery salt, and salt together in a medium bowl until the sugar and salt are dissolved. Stir in the capers.

Make a few alternating layers of the shrimp, bell pepper, onion, and candied peppers (or sugar and red pepper flakes) in a 1-quart glass container; slip in the remaining bay leaf about halfway through. Give the marinade a big stir and pour it over the shrimp and vegetables so it covers them completely. Poke anything that sticks out back into the marinade. Screw the lid on tightly and place the container in the fridge for 24 hours, flipping the jar occasionally.

To serve, drain the shrimp and vegetables completely. Put them in a shallow serving bowl or on a platter and serve with a shot glass filled with toothpicks.

NOTE

• Cooking shrimp in their shells and peeling them afterward may take a few extra minutes, but that time pays off in flavor and a dividend of shrimp broth.

• This amount of shrimp, vegetables, and marinade fits beautifully into a 1-quart canning jar. The recipe can be doubled easily to feed a larger crowd.

Auggie's Fennel-Bourbon
CANDIED HOT PEPPERS

STEPHEN • *Every night when I am in the hair-and-makeup chair for* The Late Show, *the Glam Squad and I watch one recipe from Ina Garten's show and talk about cooking. I was waxing on one night about my love of candied tangerine rinds (see page 244) when my hair stylist, Jenna Robinson, said a neighbor of hers, AJ "Auggie" Russo (proprietor of Brooklyn's Tiny Pizza Kitchen), candies hot peppers and would I like some? I would like some, and then I loved some. It became my go-to for a sweet heat in any dish: the candying process tones down the spice while leaving a smooth warm essence. And if you like peppers, they make a crispy nibble all by themselves.*

EVIE • *Unlike every other receipt in this book, this one makes an ingredient, not a dish. We have included it here (thank you, Auggie!) because we love it so much that we've listed it as an ingredient in three different dishes. It's admittedly a complicated process, but once you have made the candied chilies, they keep for a very long time. Still, if you are daunted by the idea of a multistep, possibly multiday, preparation, you can simply substitute red pepper flakes and a healthy pinch of sugar in the recipes that call for them.*

Makes about 3 cups

6 tablespoons whole fennel seeds

6 cups demerara sugar

4 cups good bourbon

Fine sea salt

3 tablespoons ground fennel (store-bought)

1 pound finger chilies

Toast the whole fennel seeds in a dry skillet until fragrant. Set aside to cool, then grind fairly coarse in a coffee or spice grinder.

Combine 4 cups of the sugar with the bourbon in a tall, narrow pot. Add a pinch of salt, 2 tablespoons of the ground toasted fennel, and 1 tablespoon of the store-bought ground fennel. Bring to a simmer over medium-low heat, stirring occasionally, until the sugar is completely dissolved.

Meanwhile, rinse the chilies and remove the stems. Slice each chili lengthwise in half. Leave in or remove as many of the seeds as you want, depending on how much heat you're looking for (the more seeds, the hotter).

continued ⟶

Once the sugar has completely dissolved, add the chilies to the pot of sugar syrup and simmer for 25 minutes. Remove from the heat.

Set a wire rack over a baking sheet. Remove the chilies with a slotted spoon or tongs and place them in a single layer—without touching—on the rack. If necessary, use a second rack/baking sheet setup. Using a fine mesh skimmer or sieve, scoop out and save any remaining fennel seed bits and chili seeds from the sugar syrup and save them to use below. Reserve the syrup for another use; see the Tips.

To season the candied chilies, mix together 1 tablespoon of the ground toasted fennel and 1 tablespoon of the store-bought ground fennel in a small bowl, then sprinkle the chilies with the mix.

Heat the oven to 150°F with a rack in the center position. Bake for 60 minutes, rotating the pan once about halfway through. The chilies should feel slightly tacky, not wet to the touch. If they don't, let them go another 5 to 10 minutes.

While the chilies are baking, spread out the reserved fennel seed bits and chili seeds in a shallow bowl. Add the remaining 1 tablespoon store-bought ground fennel, any remaining ground toasted fennel seeds, and the remaining 2 cups sugar and mix well. (You will use this mixture to coat the hot chilies after their first stint in the oven.)

Remove the chilies from the oven and, working quickly, add them to the sugar/fennel mixture in batches, turning to coat each one completely. Return them to the wire rack and continue baking for about 4 to 5 hours, rotating the pan every 30 minutes, until the chilies are completely crisp and dry when cool. If using an oven to dry the coated chilies, prop the oven door partly open with a wooden spoon to let some of the moisture escape. Pinch one from the rack and cool a few minutes to test. (Alternatively, dry the chilies for 25 to 30 hours in a dehydrator.) Store the chilies in a tightly covered container—a large canning jar with lid works well—in a cool dark place for up to a few months.

Hot CRABMEAT DIP

STEPHEN • *This recipe was a mainstay of our childhood in Charleston. It was at every party, and for good reason. It has something from all the major party food groups: hot, salty, sweet, and creamy—all on a crunchy cracker.*

EVIE • *Be careful if you serve this at your cocktail parties. You'd better put it on a large round table so there is plenty of room for all the people who will stand around eating it up.*

Makes 4 servings

Softened butter for the casserole dish

THE TOPPING

¾ cup shredded sharp cheddar cheese

⅓ cup panko

3 tablespoons finely sliced fresh chives

1 tablespoon unsalted butter, melted

THE DIP

3 tablespoons unsalted butter

3 tablespoons all-purpose flour

1 cup whole milk

1 tablespoon dry or cream sherry (optional)

Salt and cayenne pepper

1 tablespoon lemon juice

1 pound crabmeat—lump, backfin, or, if you're feeling extravagant, jumbo lump—picked over for bits of shell

Firm crackers or small toasted canapé shells for serving

Make the topping: Combine the cheddar, panko, chives, and melted butter in a small bowl and rub the mixture together. Set aside.

Make the dip: Melt the butter in a medium skillet over medium-low heat. Add the flour and whisk until the mixture is bubbly and just starting to color, about 4 minutes. Pour in the milk and sherry, if using, and bring to a simmer, whisking to keep the sauce from sticking. (Don't forget the corners of the pan!) Season with salt and cayenne pepper to taste.

Heat the broiler, on low, if that's an option, with a rack in the top position. If your broiler doesn't have a low setting, bring the rack down a level. Butter a 4-cup flameproof casserole dish and set it aside.

Remove the sauce from the heat and stir in the lemon juice. Gently fold in the crabmeat until it's evenly coated with sauce. Pour the mixture into the prepared casserole dish and sprinkle the topping evenly over it. Broil until the topping is golden brown, about 4 minutes. Let stand for a few minutes before serving.

Serve side-by-side with the crackers or canapé shells.

Warm
ARTICHOKE DIP

EVIE • *Artichoke dip might seem a bit old fashioned, but I think it is making a comeback—and in our house, it never really left. It is easy to make, a real crowd-pleaser, and, hey—you can say you are having your vegetables, just with a side of mayonnaise and cheese!*

STEPHEN • *Based on all the '70s cocktail party classics in this book, our dear friend Carrie Byalick suggested that it should be sponsored by Hellmann's and come with a mayonnaise packet bookmark. It's a fair assessment . . . or accusation, depending on how you feel about mayo. I feel strongly about it. I'm a Duke's man, myself. Besides the fact that they are a South Carolina company, it is eggier, evidenced by the fact that a newly opened jar will often have a "crack" in the mayonnaise, as if it were a custard. It also has no sugar. There is no contest, in my mayo-slathered opinion.*

Makes about 2½ cups; enough for about 30 "dips"

One 14-ounce can artichoke hearts, drained thoroughly

1 cup mayonnaise

½ cup grated Parmesan cheese

½ teaspoon garlic salt

Salt and freshly ground pepper

Paprika for sprinkling

Squares of rye bread or water crackers for serving

Heat the oven to 425°F with a rack in the center position.

Mash the drained artichoke hearts in a medium bowl to break them up into fit-on-a-cracker-sized pieces. A wooden spoon works well for this. Add the mayo, Parmesan, and garlic salt and mix in well. Add salt and pepper to taste.

Scrape the mixture into a 4-cup casserole or baking dish. Sprinkle paprika over the top and bake until the top is bubbling and light golden brown, about 15 minutes. Remove from the heat and let cool 5 to 10 minutes before serving with bread or crackers.

Claus Boils SOME PEANUTS

STEPHEN • *When Evie and I started dating (long-distance: NYC–Chicago), being exiles from the Lowcountry, one of the things we first bonded over was the local—and peculiar—food we missed. For instance: It's hard to explain the appeal of boiled peanuts to the uninitiated. They are more like a pea than a nut, which makes sense, because peanuts are technically legumes. One time, I brought green peanuts back to Chicago, boiled them up, and bagged up little packages for my comedy friends. I thought that was very generous of me, but my treats were met with broad skepticism, and word got out I was pushing a strange Southern snack on the unwary. "Oh great," they said, "here comes Colbert with more of his damp food."*

EVIE • *Our brother-in-law Claus Busch is an expert at many things, and one of them is making the perfect batch of boiled peanuts. What are boiled peanuts, you might ask? Well . . . they are peanuts that are boiled, and they are absolutely perfect on a hot summer day with a beer. As Stephen likes to say, "They taste like a creek," and in fact they are best eaten in a creek, on a boat with a beer in hand. We will now turn this over to Claus to explain the mystery behind creating a perfect batch of boiled peanuts.*

CLAUS • *Start with about 2 pounds of green peanuts (see Note). Pick out any bad peanuts—those with little bits of mold, mushy shells, etc. Wash the peanuts in the sink, the pot you'll use to boil the peanuts, or anything you can find that's large enough to give them a good cleaning. Swish them around to get any dirt off them. Place the peanuts in a large pot and pour in enough cold water to cover them. The peanuts will float, but make sure there is enough water to keep the peanuts off the bottom of the pot. Pour some salt over the peanuts and stir into the water. Start with ¼ cup salt; additional salt can be added later.*

Bring the water to a boil, then reduce to a simmer and cover the pot. Make sure the water does not boil away at any time during the cooking. Let cook for 2 hours, then taste a peanut for saltiness. (Pop it open. Don't eat the shell!) Add additional salt, if desired. Then keep cooking, checking every so often for the doneness (which depends on how soft you like your peanuts).

Turn off the heat and let the peanuts cool in the water. Drain off the water and enjoy.

NOTE

• Don't confuse green peanuts (i.e., freshly dug) with unroasted dried peanuts. Green peanuts are harvested only from August through October. They are perishable and will keep for only 5 days or so when refrigerated, although they can be frozen for longer. (However, dried unroasted peanuts will make an acceptable albeit much different kind of boiled peanut.) If you don't live near a farm that digs its own green peanuts, they are available online at sites like Hardy Farms (hardyfarmspeanuts.com).

A FEW PEANUT POINTERS FROM CLAUS

- Most green peanuts for boiling are either the Valencia or the Virginia variety.

- After boiling, I have allowed my peanuts to sit overnight in the salted water to add additional flavor.

- If you taste a few peanuts after 2 hours and find them too salty, remove some of the water, replace it with fresh (unsalted) water, and bring it back to a boil (osmosis!) before continuing.

- To make flavored peanuts, you can add spices to the water at the beginning of cooking: Old Bay and cayenne pepper, for example.

Cayenne Pepper–Pimento
CHEESE SPREAD

EVIE • *This is another of our brother-in-law Claus's receipts. Pimento cheese is a staple of the Lowcountry, and you can find it at many restaurants and some stores. But beware, some pimento cheese simply isn't good. You need the right balance of spicy and cheesiness to make it perfect. Claus has found that balance, and this is the perfect pimento cheese.*

STEPHEN • *This is where Evie and I part ways. She doesn't do deviled eggs. I don't do pimento cheese. I know it's a staple of our childhood, but I must have gotten some of that low-rent pimento as a kid.*

Makes about 2 cups

1 tablespoon cream cheese

1 tablespoon Durkee Famous Sauce (see Note)

One 4-ounce jar diced pimentos (about ⅓ cup), with their juice (or drain the juice to make a cheese ball that's a little firmer)

¼ cup mayonnaise, or more if necessary

1 teaspoon apple cider vinegar, or more to taste, or none at all

1 teaspoon prepared horseradish (coarse cut if available)

½ teaspoon freshly ground pepper

½ teaspoon garlic powder

¼ to ½ teaspoon cayenne pepper

A little grated sweet onion (optional)

6 to 8 ounces sharp yellow cheddar cheese, finely grated (2 to 2½ cups)

6 to 8 ounces sharp white cheddar cheese, finely grated (2 to 2½ cups)

Using the back of a spoon, mash the cream cheese and the Durkees together in a medium bowl. (Mixing the Durkees with the cream cheese before adding all the other ingredients keeps the cream cheese from lumping.) Stir in the pimentos, mayo, vinegar, if using, horseradish, black pepper, garlic powder, cayenne, and onion, if using, until evenly blended. Stir in the cheddar cheeses until everything is evenly mixed.

Form the mixture into a ball, or press it into the bowl you'll use for serving. The spread can be made ahead and refrigerated for up to several days. Be sure to bring it to room temperature for an hour or two before serving.

NOTE

• "Durkees" is a staple of Southern households that is somewhere between mayo and mustard. Look for it in the condiment section (even in supermarkets up North!) or order some online.

COWBOY CAVIAR

EVIE • *My friend Katie Dancy is a fantastic cook. She has shared many receipts with me over the years, all of which I love, but this might be my favorite. While there are several versions of cowboy caviar out there, the avocado and balsamic vinegar make this one exceptional. I often add even more of each because those are two of my favorite things on the planet, so why not! Stephen will deny this, but there has been more than one occasion when cowboy caviar and chips were our entire dinner.*

STEPHEN • *Why would I deny that? I would consider cowboy caviar one of our more balanced dinners, especially now that the kids are grown. Many's the night our dinner is a glass (or two) of white wine, a handful of cashews, and Anderson Cooper. Also, what is this "chips" business? I have, on more than one occasion, simply leaned over the sink and happily shoveled in the cowboy caviar with a spoon. So, yeah, we're fans.*

Makes about 4 cups; plenty for a big gathering

One 15-ounce can black-eyed peas, drained and rinsed

One 15-ounce can shoepeg corn, drained and quickly rinsed

½ pound Roma (plum) tomatoes, cored and diced about the size of the black-eyed peas (about 1½ cups)

½ cup chopped fresh cilantro, including the thinner stems if you like

4 green onions, trimmed and thinly sliced

2 cloves garlic, pressed or minced

2 tablespoons balsamic vinegar

2 tablespoons olive oil

1½ teaspoons sriracha or other hot sauce

1 to 2 avocados (depending how much you like avocados)

Salt and freshly ground pepper

Corn chips, pita chips, gluten-free crackers . . . (you get the idea)

Gently toss together the black-eyed peas, corn, tomatoes, cilantro, green onions, and garlic in a large bowl. Whisk the vinegar, oil, and sriracha together in a small bowl, pour over the caviar, and toss to mix.

If serving the caviar right away, halve, pit, and dice the avocado(s) and gently toss together with the other ingredients. If not, the caviar can be covered and stored for a few hours, or up to overnight. Bring to room temperature for about an hour and then toss in the avocado.

Either way, season the caviar with salt and pepper to taste just before serving. Serve with chips or crackers for scooping.

GREEN GODDESS DIP

EVIE • *Who doesn't like a good green goddess dip? This receipt is from our sister-in-law Kitty Colbert, and it is the best we know. Just make up a batch and keep it in the fridge. You will find yourself pulling it out for all kinds of things. It makes a great dressing for chicken salad or green salad, a sandwich spread, and a fantastic dip for crudités or the Chickpea Fries on page 52.*

STEPHEN • *I had always thought Green Goddess was a '70s industrial food flavor, like Fresca, dreamed up by the boys in the salad labs at Seven Seas. But Kitty opened my eyes and mouth to the original, which I was surprised to learn is over a hundred years old. In 1923, the chef of the Palace Hotel in San Francisco, Philip Roemer, whipped it up in honor of the English actor George Arliss and named it for his play,* The Green Goddess. *Thanks, Phil. You made crudités edible.*

Makes about 1¼ cups

½ cup mayonnaise

½ cup sour cream

¼ cup chopped green onion tops

2 to 4 tablespoons chopped fresh chives

2 tablespoons chopped fresh flat-leaf parsley

Juice of 1 lemon

1½ teaspoons chopped fresh tarragon

¾ teaspoon anchovy paste or 1 to 2 anchovy fillets

Salt if needed

Seasonal vegetables (especially asparagus!), cut into dipping shapes, and/or crackers, chips, or any of your favorite dippers

Put all the ingredients except the vegetables and/or dippers into the bowl of a food processor or a blender jar and process until smooth and light green, at least 60 seconds; stop to scrape down the bowl or jar once or twice. Taste and add salt if necessary. Scrape into a bowl and refrigerate until ready to serve.

Serve the dip with vegetables, crackers, and/or chips. The dip will keep in the refrigerator for 4 or 5 days.

Notes

The dates can be pitted, stuffed, and wrapped well in advance and stored in the freezer. Freeze them on a tray, and once they are frozen, transfer them to a sealable plastic bag.

•

You can bake the dates almost fully before the party and then finish them up when guests arrive.

BACON-WRAPPED DATES
Stuffed with Marcona Almonds

EVIE • *Our friend Sherry Pincus is a caterer extraordinaire. Unfortunately for us, she has retired and traded in her chef's hat for a backpack and hiking boots. But for a while, there she was, the magic behind every Colbert party. Our friends got to know Sherry so well that they would sneak into the kitchen to grab her hors d'oeuvres fresh out of the oven. These bacon-wrapped dates are our absolute favorite. They make the house smell terrific and put you in a party mood immediately. Good luck passing them around, though—if your house is like ours, they will get gobbled up instantly. The sweet-smoky-crunchy is a total crowd-pleaser.*

STEPHEN • *That last part is referring to me. Whenever Sherry made these for a party at our house, Evie would catch me in the kitchen hovering over a tray of the little flavor grenades, waiting for them to cool enough so I could pop them into my mouth like seedless grapes.*

Makes 60 dates (recipe can be easily halved)

30 Medjool dates, preferably pitted (but pitting them yourself isn't the end of the world)
1 pound bacon (not thick-cut)
60 roasted unsalted Marcona almonds (about 1 cup)

You'll need toothpicks or fancy smallish wooden skewers.

Heat the oven to 350°F with a rack in the center position. Line a rimmed baking sheet with aluminum foil or parchment paper.

If you need to pit your dates, use needle-nose pliers to go in at one end of each date and grab hold of the pit, then pull gently but firmly to remove it. Or, using a paring knife, slice open each date lengthwise and fish out the pit. (Once you get the hang of either method, the work goes fairly quickly.) Cut the dates crosswise in half.

Cut the bacon strips crosswise in half and then lengthwise in half. Tuck an almond into the center of each date half, but leave a little of it poking out. Wrap a cut strip of bacon around the middle of each date half and secure the end of the strip with a toothpick or skewer. Line up the wrapped dates on the prepared baking sheet. This can be done in advance; cover and refrigerate until needed, or up to 12 hours.

Bake the dates until the bacon is crispy and the dates are jammy, about 25 minutes. Turn them over halfway through so the bacon and bottoms of the dates don't burn. These will be screamin' hot right out of the oven, so give them 5 to 10 minutes to cool down a little.

Dad's DEVILED EGGS

EVIE • *My mother was the real cook in our family, but there were a few things that my dad loved to make, and deviled eggs was one of them, which is so helpful, because, honestly, who wants to clean a hard-boiled egg if they don't have to? Our family always has a big 4th of July party, and Dad's deviled eggs are such a crowd-pleaser that sometimes they are gone before he even gets to eat one—so now we hold back a few in the kitchen just for him!*

STEPHEN • *I love my father-in-law, and I love his deviled eggs. In fact (because I seem to have a role here as something of a fact checker), I love the deviled eggs more than Evie does. She doesn't eat them. You may have noticed that in the paragraph above, she says that they are a "crowd-pleaser." She doesn't say they're an "Evie-pleaser." I think they are too close to egg salad, which is always a hard pass from Miss McGee.*

Makes 24 deviled eggs

12 large eggs

1 cup mayonnaise

1 small yellow onion, finely diced (about ⅓ cup)

2 teaspoons Dijon mustard

2 teaspoons white wine vinegar

Salt and freshly ground pepper

Paprika for sprinkling

Bring a large pot of water to a boil, carefully slip in all 12 eggs, and boil for 10 minutes. Meanwhile, fill a large bowl with ice and water. When the eggs are done, lift them out with a slotted spoon and place in the ice bath to cool completely. Drain.

Peel the eggs and cut them lengthwise in half. Scoop out the yolks into a medium bowl. Add the mayonnaise, onion, mustard, and vinegar and beat with a whisk or a handheld mixer until smooth (except, of course, for the onion). Season with salt and pepper, starting with ½ teaspoon salt and 1 teaspoon pepper and adjusting from there as you like.

Spoon the filling neatly into the egg white halves (or use a piping bag fitted with a wide tip, so the onions don't get stuck). Sprinkle a little paprika over the filling.

The deviled eggs can be made up to several hours ahead of time. Cover them very loosely and refrigerate until serving.

Sivvy Bean
HUMMUS

STEPHEN • *Not everybody is a fan of lima beans—or, in the Lowcountry, butter beans or "sivvy" beans (if they are small). I love them with just butter and salt, and if you can find them freshly shelled, it makes all the difference. This sivvy hummus, green and bright, is sure to please even the most lima-leery.*

EVIE • *It's true! This sivvy bean hummus is in the same category as carrot cake—don't let the name put you off. It is a creamy and light version of hummus that you will love.*

Makes about 1¾ cups

2 cups (about 12 ounces) lima beans (fresh if possible, defrosted frozen baby limas if not)

2 cloves garlic

Juice of ½ lemon

2 tablespoons tahini

¼ cup extra-virgin olive oil, or as needed

½ teaspoon salt

Pita chips, sturdy crackers, and/or vegetables cut into dippable-sized pieces

Combine all the ingredients except the chips, etc., in a food processor and pulse until smooth. If the hummus seems too dry, drizzle in additional olive oil and pulse until it becomes smooth. Serve with pita chips, crackers, and/or sliced veggies.

Courgette
"MADELEINES"

STEPHEN • *In the interest of full disclosure, I'll jump in here to say that our daughter's name is Madeleine. No relation.*

EVIE • *While we were vacationing in Provence in the summer of 2022, we met Jane Satow. Jane is an American ex-pat who now lives near Saint-Rémy-de-Provence and runs a cooking school, La Cuisine Provençale. She is a wonderful chef and, thanks to her, our trip was a gastronomical triumph! Jane helped us with restaurant reservations, cooked for us, and led us in cooking classes as well. She has graciously allowed us to share a couple of the receipts she taught us. We are so happy to share them with you, as they provide a glimpse into Provençal cooking and are truly unique and delicious. I will let Jane take it from here:*

JANE SATOW • *There are dozens of different recipes using zucchini in Provence, from deep-frying the flowers to a gratin de courgettes. There are also quite a few savory cake recipes, which are usually made in a loaf tin and sliced, to be served before dinner with drinks—a time-honored tradition in France, affectionately referred to as* l'apéro.

I developed this savory madeleine recipe using zucchini as a lighter alternative to the traditional savory French cake recipes, which often call for bacon or ham. The size of the madeleines is perfect for serving at a cocktail party as finger food, but you can also make them in a mini-muffin pan.

Making a savory cake is very much like making a sweet cake, only with no sugar. There is just one secret to making madeleines that diverges from any other cake recipe and that is achieving la petite chapeau—*the little pop-up hat on top of the madeleine—which is created by placing the madeleines into the fridge for at least 35 to 45 minutes before baking them. The top pops up because of the shock of difference in temperature when the cold batter goes into the hot oven, and voilà: poof!*

continued ⟶

Makes 12 mini-muffins or twelve 3-inch madeleines

Softened butter for the pan if not using a silicone or nonstick madeleine tin

¾ cup all-purpose flour, sifted, plus more for the muffin tin or the madeleine tin if not using a silicone or nonstick tin

1 cup loosely packed grated raw zucchini (from about 2 small zucchini; smaller zukes are better)

2 tablespoons crème fraîche

½ teaspoon salt, preferably fleur de sel from the Camargue

½ teaspoon baking powder

½ teaspoon baking soda

1 large egg

2 tablespoons extra-virgin olive oil

1 teaspoon coarsely ground pepper

1 teaspoon herbes de Provence

2 tablespoons finely grated Parmesan cheese

You'll need a mini-muffin tin or a standard madeleine mold.

tip—If you can find silicone molds, they are fab, eliminating the need for buttering and flouring them.

If you're using a muffin tin or regular madeleine mold (not silicone or nonstick), butter the pan and dust lightly with flour.

Stir together the grated zucchini and crème fraîche in a small bowl. In another small bowl, stir together the sifted flour, salt, baking powder, and baking soda.

In a medium bowl, beat the egg with a handheld mixer or a whisk until light and fluffy, about 1 minute. While beating (or whisking), drizzle in the olive oil and continue beating until the mixture is pale yellow and doubled in volume. Gently fold in the zucchini and dry ingredients a bit at a time until just incorporated.

Spoon the batter into the tin and sprinkle the tops of the madeleines with the pepper, herbes de Provence, and grated cheese. Let the batter rest, uncovered, in the fridge for at least 30 minutes, and up to 2 hours.

Heat the oven to 350°F with a rack in the center position. Bake the madeleines straight from the refrigerator until golden brown, 8 to 10 minutes. If you press on the center of a madeleine, it should spring right back. Let the madelelines cool in the pans for 10 minutes, then unmold and serve warm.

CHICKPEA FRIES
(Panelle)

EVIE • *I can't remember the first time Stephen made these—probably one cold Saturday afternoon in the winter when he was feeling creative and found chickpea flour in our cupboard. All I know is that I love them. They are lighter than potato fries but still decadent and satisfying. A perfect snack with an aioli or Green Goddess Dip (page 40).*

STEPHEN • *In 2012, my doctor threatened me with cholesterol medicine or a change of diet. I chose the new diet. "No carbs! No bread, no rice, no sugar, no potatoes." Deal. I figured as long as I could have coffee in the morning and a glass of wine at night, I could eat bark and rusty nails in between. I was monastic about it for seven months, I lost 17 pounds, and my cholesterol did not move an inch. Drugs ahoy! These "fries" were discovered in one of my poorly thought-out attempts to get around doctor's orders. Sadly, it turns out chickpeas are not, as I'd assumed, low-carb; in fact, pound for pound, they have way more carbs than russet potatoes. I don't know where I heard that. I assume, in the depths of French fry withdrawal, I just hallucinated the nutritional info I wanted. Thankfully, being wrong has never tasted so right, because I discovered the simple, delicious joy of panelle.*

This recipe makes quite a bit, but you can either halve the ingredients or do what I do—make the mix and keep it refrigerated, cooking up batches of fries over the course of a few days.

Makes about 50 "fries"

2 tablespoons extra-virgin
olive oil, plus more for the pan

2 cups chickpea flour

2½ teaspoons salt, plus more
for sprinkling

1½ teaspoons garlic powder
(optional)

1 teaspoon freshly ground
pepper

4 cups cold water

Vegetable or canola oil for
shallow-frying

Lemon wedges

Coat a 9 × 12-inch baking dish with olive oil and set aside.

Sift the chickpea flour into a 3- to 4-quart saucepan. Add the salt, garlic powder, if using, and the pepper. Pour the cold water into the flour in a slow stream, whisking constantly. (Sifting the chickpea flour and starting with cold water increase your chances of having a lump-free batter.) Whisk in the 2 tablespoons olive oil. Heat over medium-low heat, whisking steadily, until the mixture starts to thicken up (this will happen quickly). Switch to a heatproof spatula or wooden spoon and cook, stirring constantly so the mixture doesn't stick and scorch, until it comes to a boil. Cook for 1 minute, stirring and scraping constantly and paying special attention to the corners of the pan.

Scrape the batter into the prepared baking dish and smooth out the top—an offset spatula dipped in water works nicely for this. Cool at room temperature for at least an hour before popping the batter into the fridge to set up and chill for at least 30 minutes, and up to 2 days, before cutting.

Once the batter has set, cut all of it, or as much of it as you plan to use, into good-sized batons, about 3 × ½ × ½ inch. Cover and refrigerate any batter you won't be using now.

Pour ½ inch of vegetable oil into a large skillet and heat until a corner of a "fry" gives off a very lively sizzle when lowered into the oil. (If you have a deep-fry or instant-read thermometer, the temperature should be around 350°F.) Carefully slide as many fries into the hot oil as fits without crowding. Cook until the undersides are a nice golden brown, about 3 minutes. Flip and repeat on the second side. Adjust the heat as necessary throughout the frying so the oil sizzles nicely.

With a slotted spoon, move the fries from the oil to a paper towel–lined plate. (If you like, keep the fries warm in a 200°F oven on a paper towel–lined baking sheet while you cook the remaining fries.) Repeat with another batch of fries, but make sure the oil is back to temperature before you start frying them.

Sprinkle the golden-brown fries with salt and serve with lemon wedges or any dipping sauce that tickles your fancy.

LEMON-CHICKEN-
ORZO SOUP
60

STEPHEN'S
KINDERGARTEN SOUP
62

HANDMADE
TOMATO SOUP
65

CLAM CHOWDER
66

EMERGENCY
CORN CHOWDER
71

LENTIL SOUP
74

DAD'S OKRA SOUP
77

MUSHROOM-
PARSNIP SOUP
79

SOUPS

One of my earliest memories of cooking comes from kindergarten. My little school was the Martin Luther Kindergarten (to the chagrin of my very Catholic parents). The teachers scared me, but there was a very friendly cook, and often she would have us help her make the hot lunch. It was simple tasks, like snapping peas, but it was more fun than being forced to nap on a scrap of rug, and it always felt special to be called up to the counter to help.

It was also a sly way of getting us to do schoolwork, because after we made the lunch, the cook would have us write down the ingredients and do little drawings of them. The recipe on page 62 is one of those assignments I brought home, which my mother promptly framed.

Ingredients: Carrot, Onion, Potato, Celery, Steve, Tomato, Okra, Corn, Butter beans, Green beans, Peas. And Meat. The generic nature of that last ingredient is somewhat off-putting, so let's say . . . beef?

Mom had this on her wall for years, and she would occasionally make the soup adhering to the list, guessing the amounts and improvising the complete lack of instructions. It was good.

That's one of the things I like about soup. It's very forgiving. If you know what you're doing, you can often just throw together ingredients and walk away while the bubbling does a lot of the work. But if you have only a general idea of what you're attempting, you can find your way, nudging the pot along one ingredient at a time.

None of the soups to follow are particularly complicated, and several of them are from pure improvisation based on available ingredients or vivid memories of past meals, including that vegetable soup I drew at age five.

So, I don't remember her name, but I'd like to thank the kindergarten cook who called me up to the counter that day. And for teaching me all those gospel songs, but that's another book. • STEPHEN

LEMON-CHICKEN-ORZO SOUP

EVIE • *This is another Katie Dancy receipt. Katie could heal the world with this delicious, soul-satisfying soup. I am so happy that she has allowed me to share it—now the world will be a better place. Make this soup for your friends and neighbors, and they will love you even more than they already do.*

STEPHEN • *I've never had this. Looks good, though.*

EVIE • *I guess that means I heal Stephen in other ways.*

Makes about 3 quarts; 6 large or 12 smaller servings

¼ cup olive oil

4 medium carrots, peeled and diced

3 stalks celery, trimmed and diced

1 medium or 2 small onions, diced

4 cloves garlic, sliced or minced

Salt and freshly ground pepper

1 teaspoon chopped fresh thyme

½ teaspoon red pepper flakes

5 cups chicken broth, homemade or store-bought

½ cup orzo

1 tablespoon good-quality chicken bouillon base, such as Better Than Bouillon

3 cups shredded cooked chicken breast meat (see sidebar if you want to cook your own chicken)

1 cup half-and-half

1 cup packed chopped spinach

½ cup grated Parmesan cheese

Grated zest and juice of 2 lemons

Heat the olive oil in a 5- to 6-quart Dutch oven or other heavy pot over medium-low heat. Stir in the carrots, celery, onions, and garlic, season lightly with salt and pepper, and cook until the vegetables are wilted and the onions are tender, about 10 minutes. Stir in the thyme and red pepper flakes and cook until fragrant, about 2 minutes.

Pour in the chicken broth and bring to a boil. Reduce the heat slightly, stir in the orzo and bouillon, and cook for 10 minutes. Add the shredded chicken, half-and-half, spinach, and Parmesan cheese and simmer for 5 minutes.

Taste the soup for seasoning and thickness. If it's too thick, add more water, season again, and bring to a simmer. If it's too thin, continue simmering for a few minutes longer, until the consistency feels right. Just before serving, stir in the lemon zest and juice.

vegan variation

Omit the chicken, half-and-half, and Parmesan cheese. Add 1 cleaned and chopped leek (white and light green parts only) to the carrots, celery, and onion in the pan. Substitute 5 cups water plus 3 tablespoons Better Than Boullion Roasted Garlic Base or 5 cups vegetable broth for the chicken broth. Add one 14-ounce can full-fat coconut milk along with the broth.

SIMPLE COOKED CHICKEN BREAST FOR SOUPS AND SALADS

To end up with about 3 cups shredded or diced cooked chicken breast, start with 1½ pounds boneless, skinless chicken breasts. Heat the oven to 400°F with a rack in the top position. Season the chicken breasts liberally with salt and pepper and a drizzle of olive oil, rubbing the seasonings into the chicken. Put the chicken on a rimmed baking sheet and bake until cooked through (165°F in the center of the thickest part), 20 to 30 minutes depending on the thickness of the breasts. Cool the chicken completely, then shred or cut as called for in the recipe.

Stephen's
KINDERGARTEN SOUP

STEPHEN • *This is the vegetable soup featured in the intro to this chapter. Here I'm making it with chuck or round and beef broth. Feel free to substitute the meat of your choice. All the amounts in this recipe—and the vegetables themselves—are just guidelines. Use whatever you like most. If you go overboard on the amount of vegetables and they're poking out of the top of the soup, just add enough beef broth or water to barely cover them and keep on going. As I said in the chapter intro, my mom would occasionally take this recipe down off the wall to cook a batch, and she always remarked on the enormous amount it would make. So if you don't end up with a lot of it, you've done something wrong.*

EVIE • *Stephen and his mom had a wonderfully close relationship. It makes me so happy to think about Lorna making this kindergarten soup for her youngest child. I have never tried to make it, because it is something special that they shared, but I have the receipt framed and hung on our wall. I think LOVE is the main ingredient here.*

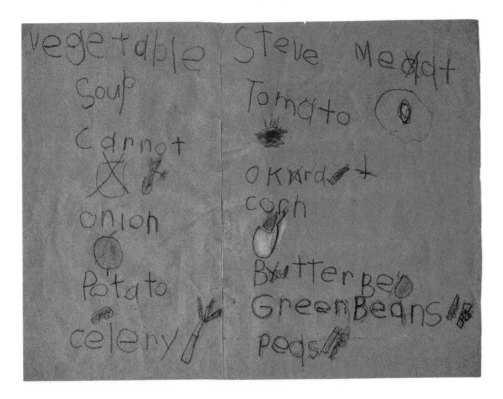

¼ cup vegetable oil or
4 tablespoons (½ stick) butter,
or a mix of the two

1 pound boneless beef chuck
or round, cut into spoon-sized
pieces

1 onion, diced

2 stalks celery, trimmed and
diced

2 medium carrots, peeled and
diced

4 cups beef broth, homemade
or store-bought

One 15-ounce can diced
tomatoes, with their liquid

½ pound okra, topped and
cut into ¾-inch-wide slices
(about 1 cup)

Salt and freshly ground
pepper

1 russet or Yukon Gold potato,
peeled and cut into large
cubes (about 2 cups)

Kernels from 2 ears corn
(about 2 cups; see Tip on
page 72) or 2 cups frozen corn

1½ pounds butter beans in the
shell, shelled (about 1½ cups)
or 1½ cups frozen lima beans

¼ pound green beans,
trimmed and cut into
spoon-sized pieces

1 cup shelled fresh peas or
frozen peas

Heat the oil and/or butter in a large (about 8-quart) Dutch oven or other heavy pot over medium-high heat until hot. Add the beef and cook, stirring occasionally, until lightly browned. If it looks like the beef is steaming more than it is browning, turn up the heat and wait for the liquid to cook off and the beef to start browning. Scoop the beef out into a bowl.

Add the onion, celery, and carrots to the pot and cook, stirring, until the vegetables are wilted, a few minutes. Return the beef to the pot, pour in the beef broth, and add the tomatoes and okra. Bring to a boil, then reduce the heat to a simmer and skim off any foam that has bubbled to the top. Taste and add salt and pepper as needed. Cook for 20 to 30 minutes, until you can feel the beef starting to soften and the whole bubbling pot start to really come together.

Stir in the potato, corn, butter beans, and green beans. Cook until this latest addition of vegetables is al dente and the beef is tender, about 20 minutes. Stir in the peas and cook for 5 to 10 minutes to bring it all together.

Season the soup one last time and ladle it into mugs or bowls. Serve with some crusty bread and butter. This soup will keep in the refrigerator for up to 5 days, and it freezes beautifully.

Handmade
TOMATO SOUP

STEPHEN • *Growing up, if any of us kids were out sick from school, Mom would give us cinnamon toast and ginger ale during the day, and if we felt better at dinner time, some tomato soup with saltine crackers. For me, that will always be the taste and smell of care. Mom's tomato soup recipe was very simple: open a can of Campbell's. (And if you don't add the can of milk, it makes a great sauce for those Mrs. Paul's fish sticks every Friday in Lent.)*

EVIE • *Although this is, in fact, a handmade tomato soup, it is also a fine soup for marinating your hands. (See book cover.)*

Makes 5 cups; 3 to 4 servings

3 tablespoons extra-virgin olive oil or unsalted butter, or a mix of the two

1 medium yellow onion, diced

2 cloves garlic, sliced

One 28-ounce can diced tomatoes, with their liquid

1 cup vegetable or chicken broth, homemade or store-bought

½ cup packed fresh basil leaves, plus finely shredded basil, for garnish

½ cup heavy cream

Salt and freshly ground pepper

Heat the olive oil and/or butter in a 2-quart saucepan over medium-low heat. Add the onion and garlic, cover the pan, and cook until the onion is softened, about 10 minutes. Check on it a couple of times—it should be simmering gently in the fat but not taking on any color.

Stir in the tomatoes and broth, bring to a simmer, and cover the pot. Simmer for about 15 minutes, then remove from the heat. Stir in the basil and let steep for 10 minutes.

Puree the soup in a regular blender, or use an immersion blender right in the pot. Add the cream and buzz the soup again. Season with salt and pepper if needed. Serve garnished with finely shredded basil leaves.

If your child is home sick from school but is now feeling a little better, give them a small bowl, maybe with a few saltines . . .

CLAM CHOWDER

STEPHEN • *In November of 2007, Evie and I were in San Francisco for an event at City Arts & Lectures, and we started our first day with an early lunch. Our host, Sydney Goldstein, had recommended The Ferry Building, a huge building on the wharf, filled with amazing local vendors of fresh and prepared foods, with several restaurants that frequently used those local ingredients in their menus.*

Suckers for shellfish, we settled in at the counter of the Hog Island Oyster Company, starting with two glasses of Sancerre. It was 11 a.m. Pacific, but we were drinking on London time. After a flight of meaty, briny oysters from up the coast, we had two Cowgirl Creamery grilled cheese sandwiches and bowls of clam chowder that were prepared fresh at the cook station right by our seats. This wasn't a creamy New England or tomato-based Manhattan chowder, but a simple, brothy soup with plenty of clam meat and vegetables that were still a bit al dente.

Maybe it was the Sancerre, but I've never enjoyed a bowl more.

Here is the recipe that I watched being made that one time and have tried to re-create many times.

EVIE • *The Sancerre and soup were both delicious, but the real secret to the dreaminess of the day was that we were on our first trip alone in years and had left our twelve-, ten-, and six-year-olds back in New Jersey. We love vacations with our children, but a get-away weekend sometimes calls for a little day drinking to celebrate.*

continued ⟶

Makes 4 servings

3 dozen small clams, such as littlenecks

2 tablespoons extra-virgin olive oil

2 stalks celery, trimmed and diced

1 medium carrot, peeled and diced

2 shallots, finely chopped

Salt

2 teaspoons fresh thyme leaves

Freshly ground pepper

3 cups vegetable broth or seafood/shrimp stock
(see Note on page 24)

1 large red potato or Yukon Gold potato
(about ½ pound), cut into ½-inch dice (about 1½ cups)

2 tablespoons unsalted butter (optional)

½ cup heavy cream

Scrub the clams under cold running water with a stiff brush, making sure to get into all the crevices. You can do this up to a day in advance and refrigerate the clams in a bowl covered with plastic wrap.

Heat the olive oil in a soup pot or large deep skillet over medium heat. When the oil is shimmering, stir in the celery, carrot, and shallots and season lightly with salt. When the shallots have started browning and the celery is beginning to turn pale, add the thyme and a few good grindings of pepper. Sauté, stirring, until you get that beautiful thyme aroma.

Stir in the broth and potato. Bring to a boil, adjust the heat to a simmer, and cook for 5 minutes. Add the clams and raise the heat to high. Cover and cook, stirring a couple of times, until the clams have opened and the potato is fork-tender, about 5 minutes. (Discard any unopened clams.)

Divide the clams among four bowls. Stir the butter and heavy cream into the broth, bring to a simmer, and cook for 1 minute. Add salt or not, as you see fit. Ladle the broth and vegetables over the clams in the bowls.

NOTE

• Make sure you have bowls handy for people to put the shells in as they scoop the clams out and into the broth.

Emergency CORN CHOWDER

EVIE • *We created this soup one winter afternoon when we'd lost power and everything in our freezer was melting. We needed to do something with a bag of frozen corn, so we sautéed it in order to bring out the sugar (the gas was still working, thank goodness). Everything else that went into the pot was also something that needed to be used, including the bacon! We were so happy with the results that now we don't wait for the power to go out.*

STEPHEN • *I'd like to point out that while Evie mentions bacon in her story above (all true), there is no bacon in her ingredient list below, because she is actually a very selective vegan—milk in her coffee, cream in her soup, butter in a cookie, fish when it's fresh, cheese when in France. Instead, she includes smoked salt in her list, which works well—but there is no proper substitute for the real thing. So, at my insistence, there is a bacon variation below the main recipe. You're welcome.*

EVIE • *I am not really a vegan—just a party pooper when it comes to meat. And for what it is worth, I think this is equally delicious using smoked salt instead of the brined swine!*

continued →

Makes 11 to 12 cups; 6 large or
10 smaller servings

3 tablespoons olive oil

One 10-ounce bag frozen corn
or the kernels from 3 ears
yellow corn, 2 generous cups
(see Tip)

1 yellow onion, diced

4 cloves garlic, minced

3 tablespoons butter

3 tablespoons all-purpose
flour

5 cups vegetable broth,
homemade or store-bought

1 pound baby potatoes, cut
into ½-inch pieces (about
2 cups)

½ teaspoon fresh thyme leaves

1 teaspoon smoked salt, such
as Bulls Bay, or as needed

Freshly ground pepper

1 cup heavy cream

¼ teaspoon paprika

Salt if needed

1 bunch fresh chives, cut into
½-inch pieces (optional)

tip—If using fresh corn,
shuck the corn, removing
as much silk as possible.
Trim the stalk ends of the
ears flat. Stand each ear on
the stalk end and use a knife
to cut the kernels from the
cob. Expect some rogue
kernels taking off across
the kitchen.

Heat the olive oil in a large Dutch oven or other heavy pot over
medium-low heat. Add the corn and cook, stirring occasionally,
until nicely browned. Add the onion and garlic and cook until the
onion is translucent, 4 to 5 minutes.

Add the butter, and as soon as it is fully melted, add the flour,
stirring vigorously to avoid clumping. Continue cooking, stirring
constantly until the onion and roux take on some color, 5 to
8 minutes.

Add the vegetable broth, potatoes, and thyme and season with
the smoked salt and pepper to taste. Bring to a boil, then reduce
the heat to low, cover, and cook until the potatoes are tender,
about 10 minutes. Gently stir in the heavy cream and paprika.
Taste for seasoning—if the soup needs both smokiness and salt,
go with more of the smoked salt. If it's just missing salt, sprinkle
in some regular salt.

Ladle the chowder into mugs or bowls and top with the
chopped chives, if using. The soup will keep for up to 4 days in the
refrigerator or up to 3 months in the freezer. If it's been frozen,
you may have to add a little more liquid when reheating it.

corn and bacon variation

Cut 4 thick-cut slices of bacon crosswise into ½-inch-wide or so
strips. Add the bacon to the pot along with the onion and garlic.
You may want to reduce or eliminate the smoked salt and, if the
soup needs it, season with regular salt.

LENTIL SOUP

EVIE • *In the early '80s, my mother, sister, and I discovered* Jane Brody's Good Food Book: Living the High-Carbohydrate Way. *I was all in for the low-fat/high-carb lifestyle, and it quickly became my favorite cookbook. My sister and I would share receipts from the book all the time. This lentil soup was inspired by the one in Brody's book. I make it constantly. It is my go-to item to make for a friend who is sick or recovering from surgery. Add a loaf of fresh bread and a hunk of yummy cheese, and it's a meal.*

STEPHEN • *Evie has made a lot of this soup over the years, and every time, she says, "I'm not sure about this batch. Should I put the white wine in or leave it out? It'll be better with the cheese." It's always good, and I always vote for the wine, and it is always better with the cheese. But (and here's one of the few friction points in our marriage) I like a little more zip in my soup, so I'll secretly toss a dash of cayenne pepper—out of sight of Evie, of course.*

Makes about 10 cups; about 6 hearty or 8 smaller servings

1 pound lentils

2 tablespoons extra-virgin olive oil

3 large onions, chopped

4 carrots, peeled and chopped

Salt and freshly ground pepper

1 tablespoon coarsely chopped fresh thyme or 1 teaspoon dried thyme

8 cups chicken or vegetable broth, homemade or store-bought

One 28-ounce can diced tomatoes, with their juices

½ cup dry white wine

½ cup coarsely chopped fresh flat-leaf parsley

Good bread—the type is up to you

2 cups shredded cheddar cheese for serving (optional)

Garlic croutons for serving (optional)

Empty the bag of lentils into a sieve. Go over them and pick out anything that's not a lentil. (It happens. Rarely, but it happens.) Bounce the lentils around a couple of times to make sure you got everything. Rinse the lentils under cool water and drain thoroughly.

Heat the olive oil in a 4- to 5-quart Dutch oven or other heavy pot over medium heat. Stir in the onions and carrots and season them lightly with salt and pepper. Cook, stirring often, until the onions are wilted and the carrots are starting to soften, about 5 minutes.

Stir in the thyme, then add the broth, tomatoes, and lentils, and bring to a boil. Taste and season with salt and pepper as needed. Lower the heat to a gentle simmer (the simmer will be a little less gentle once the pot is covered). Give the soup one last stir, cover the pot, and cook until the lentils are tender, about 45 minutes. Check about 5 minutes in to make sure the heat is at the right level and the soup is at a simmer.

Stir in the wine and parsley and season with more salt and pepper if you think it's needed. Cook for 5 minutes more.

Ladle the soup into bowls and serve with the bread and a sprinkle of grated cheese on top. Pass a bowl of croutons.

Dad's
OKRA SOUP

EVIE • *Okra was brought to the United States via the transatlantic slave trade, and we owe the Gullah Geechee culture of the South Carolina Sea Islands deep gratitude for this and many other classic dishes. This is my father's version of okra soup, which I am sure he adapted from his mother's. When I was a child, we ate a lot of okra in my family, and truth be told, I hated it! Too slimy and bristly. But I love Dad's okra soup. There is no sliminess here, just a wholesome and hearty soup. Give it a try even if you don't love okra. Be sure to use fresh okra— canned okra just isn't the same.*

STEPHEN • *There are only two ways I like okra: pickled or in Peter McGee's soup. As Evie mentions, cooked okra can be slimy, but acid will prevent that, and the diced tomatoes do the job here. I look forward to this soup every time Peter breaks out his recipe. He's had ninety-four years to perfect it.*

**Makes about 4 cups;
2 hearty servings**

1 pound beef stew meat, such as boneless chuck

Salt and freshly ground pepper

¼ cup olive oil

1 onion, chopped

4 cups chicken or beef broth, homemade or store-bought

One 15-ounce can diced tomatoes, with their juices

2 cups topped okra, cut into 1-inch lengths (from about ½ pound okra)

1 teaspoon chopped fresh marjoram

1 teaspoon chopped fresh thyme

Cut the beef into largeish soup spoon–sized pieces. Pat the beef dry and season generously with salt and pepper.

Heat the oil in a large Dutch oven or other heavy pot over medium heat. Add the beef and cook, stirring, until well browned on all sides. (You may need to cook the beef in batches to get it nice and brown.) Remove the beef from the pot and set it aside. Stir in the onion, reduce the heat to medium-low, and cook for a few minutes, until the onion picks up some color from the browned bits in the pot. Stir in the broth and tomatoes, season with salt and pepper, and bring to a boil. Stir in the okra, adjust the heat to a simmer, and cook for 45 minutes.

Return the beef to the pot. Reduce the heat to low, cover the pot, and cook, stirring every half hour or so, until the beef is very tender, about 1½ to 2 hours. About half an hour before the soup is ready, stir in the marjoram and thyme, along with additional salt and pepper to taste.

MUSHROOM-PARSNIP SOUP

STEPHEN • *I like parsnips. There, I said it. Where do I find the courage? These fragrant cousins of the carrot are a sweet and floral base in this mushroom soup. And not just any mushrooms— morels. If you don't know morels, they look like a tiny hat for a gnome. They are hard to find fresh, but dried morels work beautifully here. In fact, after you reconstitute the morels in hot water, you have a lovely dark mushroom broth you can use for part of the stock in the soup. This recipe came about like a lot of things I cook, by seeing whatever I had on hand and going from there. In this case, I had parsnips, a bag of dried morels, and some essentials of Japanese cooking: miso, soy sauce, and mirin—a sweet rice wine that my son Peter had introduced me to during our Covid cooking days. "That all sounds good to me," I thought. I hope it tastes good to you.*

EVIE • *If you are wondering who the heck just has parsnips and morels lying around their kitchen . . . , this tells you a lot about Stephen's trips to the grocery store. We might not have milk or trash bags, but we have dried morels, by God!*

DRIED MUSHROOM POINTERS

- Dried mushrooms come in all shapes, textures, and tastes. Morels are the mushroom of choice here, but dried chanterelles or porcini would work as well.

- Any type of dried mushroom must be soaked before using. To do this, put the mushrooms in a bowl and pour enough hot water over them to cover them by an inch or so. Let soak until softened, 15 to 30 minutes, depending on the mushroom.

- After lifting out the soaked mushrooms, strain the mushroom broth into another bowl. It is a good idea to line the sieve with a double thickness of cheesecloth or a coffee filter; some dried mushrooms are very sandy/gritty. Rinse the mushrooms after removing them from the broth. With strained mushroom broth and rinsed mushrooms, you're ready to go.

- Store any extra dried mushrooms in an airtight container in a cool, dark place.

continued →

1½ ounces dried morels or
other dried mushrooms (just
about any type will work;
see the sidebar for dried
mushroom pointers)

2 large parsnips (about
¾ pound)

3 tablespoons olive oil, plus
a little more for drizzling

1 teaspoon salt, plus more for
seasoning the parsnips

1 teaspoon freshly ground
pepper, plus more for
seasoning the parsnips

1 cup chicken broth,
homemade or store-bought

2 teaspoons white miso paste

1 heaping teaspoon dried
thyme

2 tablespoons unsalted butter

1 large shallot, chopped
(doesn't have to be fine)

2 tablespoons soy sauce

1 tablespoon mirin

1 tablespoon honey (or truffle
honey; see Tip)

3 cloves roasted garlic
(see Tip)

A small handful of sliced fresh
chives (optional)

Toasts for dipping

Put the dried morels in a bowl and cover with 2 cups of very hot water. Let sit for half an hour.

Peel the parsnips and quarter them lengthwise, then cut them into ½-inch chunks. Toss them into a soup pot, along with 2 tablespoons of the olive oil, season lightly with salt and pepper, and cook, covered, over medium heat, stirring occasionally. After about 15 minutes, the parsnips should be tender and browning.

Lift out the reconstituted mushrooms from the water, which will now be a dark brown broth. Squeeze the excess water from the mushrooms back into the bowl, then strain the mushroom broth through a paper towel or paper coffee filter to get out any of the grit that can often be on dried morels (see the sidebar). Set the mushrooms aside.

Add the mushroom broth to the parsnips, then add the chicken broth and simmer until hot. Add the miso and stir to dissolve it. Add the thyme, the teaspoon of salt, and the teaspoon of pepper and simmer over medium-low heat, covered, until the parsnips are soft.

Meanwhile, melt the butter in a sauté pan and add the shallot. Cook over medium heat until the shallot begins to soften, about 3 minutes. Add the morels and sauté until softened, 6 to 8 minutes. Add the soy sauce, mirin, honey, and garlic.

Once all your ingredients are nicely melded in your mushroom pan, remove about a dozen morels from the pan and set aside. Take everything else in your pan and scrape it into the parsnip pot. Immersion blend the entire thing, or let it cool a bit before putting it in a blender to puree. Once the soup is pureed and in the pot, add back the whole morels, and let simmer for 10 to 15 minutes.

Serve with a drizzle of olive oil on top.

---

tips

Cut a head of garlic in half, leaving the skin on. Generously grease a small baking dish with olive oil. Put the garlic, cut side down, in the dish and drizzle more oil over it. Roast until soft and lightly browned, 25 to 35 minutes.

Truffle honey will accentuate the rich flavor of the morels. It is fairly easy to get these days, but make sure that its flavoring is just from truffles, and not from "truffle flavoring." That tends to be a chemical perfume that is actually quite destructive to recipes.

If using a standard blender, wait until the soup cools quite a bit or blend the soup in small batches. Turning on a blender that is half-full of hot soup could blow the top off.

CRUNCHY
CORNFLAKE CHICKEN
WITH MANGO-
CILANTRO SAUCE
85

MANGO-CILANTRO
SAUCE
86

SPICY
HONEY–LEMON
CHICKEN THIGHS
89

CHICKEN
L'ORANGE
92

CURRIED
CHICKEN SALAD
95

BUNKY MAKES
SPATCHCOCKED
"YARDBIRD"
96

LEMON-PEPPER
RUB
100

DUCK BREAST
WITH FIG-ORANGE
SAUCE
102

CHICKEN THIGHS
WITH MUSTARD-
MUSHROOM SAUCE
104

SALT-AND-PEPPER
WINGS
107

LIME-MEZCAL
WINGS
108

WHOLE ROASTED
BUTTERMILK CHICKEN
110

POULTRY

When he was a boy, our son Peter learned to fry chicken. In retrospect, it seems like a hazardous thing to teach a child, but anytime they can feed themselves is a little victory.

One year, we were in Los Angeles for the Emmys, having left our children Back East with the babysitter. The moment we were getting into the limo, dressed to the nines, Evie's phone rang. It was the security company. Our fire alarm in New Jersey was going off. Firefighters were on the way.

STEPHEN • Do you remember setting the house on fire?

PETER • I remember making chicken. I don't remember how old I was, but I'd been making chicken for a few weeks, on and off, just chopping up chicken breasts and experimenting breading with different stuff, like saltines for breadcrumbs, and different mixes of egg and milk to make batter. I couldn't figure out how to get it to stick!

STEPHEN • I think you were ten.

PETER • I remember being older than that.

STEPHEN • You were into fried chicken when you were nine or ten.

PETER • No dude. No, no, bro, no. I think you're manipulating the past to get a cuter story.*

STEPHEN • Younger you doesn't make it cuter. It makes it more terrifying.

PETER • So, anyway . . . , one day I was heating up the cooking oil (our babysitter, Diana, had left or something). I turned on the heat and then forgot about it. The next thing I know, the oil started smoking like crazy, and the fire alarm went off, and Madeleine freaked out, and we just put the pot in the sink and let it cool off. Then the fire department came with a ton of trucks and walked inside in full gear, even though there's obviously no fire.

STEPHEN • Do you remember Madeleine yelling, "I'm gonna kill you, Peter!"?

PETER • I remember her saying way more than that. She was very upset, by the way.

STEPHEN • Remember anything else?

PETER • Ritz crackers worked pretty good. Saltines were terrible. Cornflakes were probably the most successful recipe. Seasoning's important. I don't know how KFC does their chicken, but it's really good.

STEPHEN • They have a proprietary blend of eleven herbs and spices.

PETER • That's what they say, but is that what it really is? I'm not frying anymore, but I do enjoy it. It's not healthy, but it is very tasty.

*****FACT CHECK:** He was fourteen.

CRUNCHY CORNFLAKE CHICKEN
with Mango-Cilantro Sauce

EVIE • *We love these crispy chicken fingers so much that we sometimes serve them as hors d'oeuvres at our parties. This receipt comes from our friend Sherry Pincus, who helped us with our family parties for years. If you cut the chicken into bite-sized pieces and serve them with the delicious mango-cilantro sauce on the side, it helps disguise the fact that you are basically serving chicken nuggets at your party.*

STEPHEN • *Sadly for us, but happily for her, Sherry has since moved to Washington State, but these crunchy little treats bring me back to many a Christmas party, trying not to get caught in the kitchen hoovering them off a tray. And asking Eddie the bartender to make sure Evie's wineglass was never empty. ("I swear I only had one glass last night, but I felt pretty tipsy!" "Huh . . .")*

* pictured on page 87

Makes 4 to 6 main-course servings, or about 30 hors d'oeuvre servings

⅓ cup slivered almonds

⅓ cup sugar

¼ cup sesame seeds

1½ tablespoons red pepper flakes

1½ tablespoons salt

8 cups cornflakes

1 cup all-purpose flour

2 large eggs

2 pounds boneless, skinless chicken breasts, cut into 1-inch-wide strips

Vegetable oil for deep-frying

Mango-Cilantro Sauce (recipe follows)

Combine the almonds, sugar, sesame seeds, red pepper flakes, and salt in a food processor and pulse until the almonds are coarsely chopped. Add the cornflakes and pulse again—just a few times—until the cornflakes are also coarsely chopped.

Set up a breading assembly line: Spread the flour out in a shallow bowl. Beat the eggs with a few drops of water in a second shallow bowl until well mixed. Spill the cornflake coating out into a third bowl. Set a cooling rack over a baking sheet at the end of the line.

Heat the oven to 200°F. Line a baking sheet with paper towels.

Working with a few strips of chicken at a time, roll them around in the flour to coat completely. Bounce them around between your hands to get rid of excess flour, then slip them into the egg. Move the strips into the cornflake coating, letting as much egg drip off the chicken as possible first to avoid gunking up the coating. Roll-press the strips around in the coating, then move them to the rack, shaking the strips a little to get rid of the excess coating.

continued ⟶

Pour about 1 inch of oil into a wide heavy skillet and heat over medium heat until a corner of a chicken strip lowered into the oil gives off a very lively sizzle (around 350°F on an instant-read thermometer). Carefully slip only as many of the strips into the oil as fit with an inch or so between them. As soon as the strips are in the oil, goose the heat under the pan a bit to keep the oil nice and hot. Fry, turning once, until the chicken is well browned and cooked through, 6 to 8 minutes. Remove the cooked chicken to the lined baking sheet and place it in the oven to stay warm while you fry the rest of the strips. As you cook the chicken, use a slotted spoon or wire skimmer to get rid of as many little crumbs as you can from the oil after each batch, and adjust the heat as necessary so the chicken gives off the same sizzle throughout the frying.

Serve the chicken hot or warm, but definitely while the coating is still crunchy. Dab some mango-cilantro sauce onto each plate or pass a bowl of it around the table.

Mango-Cilantro Sauce

This can be used as a dipping sauce for things like shrimp and chicken or brushed on foods toward the end of grilling.

Makes about 2½ cups

2 cups diced ripe mango

4 jalapeños, halved, seeded, and chopped

¼ cup white wine vinegar

¼ cup sugar

2 shallots, finely diced

2 tablespoons water

¼ cup chopped fresh cilantro

2 tablespoons lime juice

4 cloves garlic, minced

Salt and freshly ground pepper

Combine the mango, jalapeños, vinegar, sugar, shallots, and water in a 2-quart saucepan and bring to a boil. Reduce the heat to a simmer, cover the pan, and simmer until the mango is softened, about 10 minutes. Remove from the heat. Let the mango mixture cool slightly before pureeing it in a blender, or use an immersion blender to puree it while still hot, then let cool.

Stir the cilantro, lime juice, and garlic into the cooled puree. Add salt and pepper to taste. This keeps in the refrigerator for up to 1 week.

Spicy Honey–Lemon
CHICKEN THIGHS

STEPHEN • *This dish, part of our regular repertoire for years, came from an email from some cooking site I didn't sign up for (Yummly, maybe?). Normally I throw spam away without ever reading it, but this time I must have been bored and stuck someplace without a cell signal, because I read it, tossed it in the trash, and then made this dish from memory that night. It has changed considerably over the years of repetition and, more importantly, from sharing it back and forth with our daughter, Maddie, who now uses it as her go-to for a quick and easy crowd-pleaser. Because (up till now) neither of us has written down our versions, we often FaceTime to remind each other what the "recipe" calls for: "Hey, does this look like enough lemon? Do I have to bake it? When does the honey go in?" I think our answers change every time, but every time it works!*

MADDIE • *It's true, this is my go-to dish if I'm trying to convince people I'm a somewhat good cook. But I almost always scrap the onions—I find they often burn (that can't possibly be my fault, right?) and take on the lemon flavor in a way that's overpowering. Instead, I like to bake the chicken in a cast-iron skillet at 450°F for 15 minutes on each side. I then take the chicken out and pour half of the mixed olive oil, lemon, honey, oregano, salt, and pepper over everything. I put the chicken back into the oven for 3-ish minutes just so it bakes a little longer with that goodness on top, and then take it out of the oven and remove the chicken from the cast-iron. Using a spatula, I scrape up all the drippings, etc., in the pan, pour in the remaining olive oil/lemon/ honey mixture, and let it simmer for 2 minutes on the stovetop. The chicken goes back in the pan, I flip the thighs over a few times, and I'm done. I prefer to use chicken thighs for this, because I'm a dark-meat girl. I think the hot honey is key, but since I somehow never have it in my kitchen, I eyeball a few shakes of red pepper flakes instead.*

STEPHEN • *At the risk of enraging my daughter, we are gonna do this my way—none of that oven nonsense—in a skillet on the stove. And I keep the onions. Don't tell Maddie.*

continued →

Makes 4 servings

¼ cup olive oil

4 medium bone-in,
skin-on chicken thighs
(about 1½ pounds)

1 teaspoon salt, plus more for
seasoning the chicken

Freshly ground pepper

Grated zest and juice
of 2 lemons

2 tablespoons hot honey
or 2 tablespoons regular
honey plus ½ teaspoon red
pepper flakes

3 cloves garlic, finely diced or
crushed

1 teaspoon dried oregano

1 large onion, coarsely diced

Heat 1 tablespoon of the olive oil in a large skillet over medium-high heat. Generously season the chicken thighs with salt and pepper on both sides and lay them skin side down in the hot oil. Leave them there, undisturbed, for about 12 minutes, until the skin is crisp.

Meanwhile, make the sauce mixture: Combine the remaining 3 tablespoons olive oil, the lemon zest and juice, hot honey (or honey/red pepper flakes mix), garlic, oregano, and the 1 teaspoon salt.

When the skin has crisped up, remove the chicken to a plate and add the onion to the hot pan. Stir the onion around a bit to coat with the drippings, then place the chicken bone side down over the onion. Leave the chicken over the heat for 10 minutes, or until fully cooked (165°F on an instant-read thermometer; see the sidebar).

Move the chicken to a plate, leaving the onion and drippings behind. Reduce the heat to low and pour the sauce mixture into the pan. It will foam up immediately. Stir to deglaze the pan, then simmer the sauce until thickened. Place the chicken back in the pan and turn to coat.

Serve the chicken with the pan sauce spooned over the top.

THE THERMOMETER AND YOU

An instant-read thermometer is an easy way to tell if meats and poultry are cooked to the right temperature. It comes in handy for a lot of other things as well, like double-checking the temperature when making the Colbert Fudge on pages 253–56. Instant-read thermometers range in price from a few bucks to $150 or more. (We can assure you that you won't need a $150 thermometer for anything in this book.) Even the less-expensive models work very well, but do choose a model with a digital (as opposed to a dial) readout.

CHICKEN L'ORANGE

STEPHEN • *My mother was never taught how to cook as a girl, and raising eleven children did not leave her a lot of time to learn. The '50s and '60s were the dawn of processed foods, and they suited Mom just fine. That said, we always sat down to dinner, and were drilled on proper table manners, and she did have a few excellent dishes. This one was my favorite—the one I would ask for on my birthday and the one Mom made when the McGees came to dinner the night after Evie and I were engaged. I don't know where my mom got this recipe, but, as her recipe box is full of clippings from magazine ads, I would not be surprised if she read it on the back of a bottle of chili sauce.*

EVIE • *Early in our marriage, I asked Stephen what his favorite meal was that his mother made when he was a kid. I wanted to make it for him. This was it! I tried several times to make it, but it was never quite right. So I got insecure about it and quit making it for a while. Eventually I made a few adjustments, and though I have never been able to make it quite the way his mother did, he likes this version just as well. At least that is what he tells me, and I don't want to know if it isn't the truth.*

Makes 4 servings

¼ cup all-purpose flour

3 pounds chicken parts, preferably bone-in, skin-on

Salt and freshly ground pepper

¼ cup vegetable or canola oil

1 cup orange juice

½ cup bottled chili sauce

2 tablespoons molasses

2 tablespoons soy sauce

1 teaspoon Dijon mustard

1 teaspoon garlic salt

3 oranges, cut into wheels, for garnish

Cooked rice for serving

Heat the oven to 350°F with a rack in the center position. Spread the flour on a plate. Pat the chicken pieces dry and season them well with salt and pepper. Roll the chicken pieces in the flour to coat them lightly.

Heat the oil in a wide skillet over medium heat. The oil is ready when a chicken piece lowered into the oil gives off a very lively sizzle. Working in batches, brown the chicken on all sides—don't overcrowd the pan! Adjust the heat as necessary so the chicken keeps sizzling, without splattering. Move the cooked chicken pieces to a paper towel–lined plate to drain.

While the chicken is browning, stir the orange juice, chili sauce, molasses, soy sauce, mustard, and garlic salt together in a small bowl.

When all the chicken is cooked, pour off the fat from the pan but leave the brown crunchy bits behind. Return the pan to the heat and pour in the orange juice mixture. Bring to a boil, scraping the bottom of the pan, and simmer for 3 minutes. Remove from the heat.

Put the chicken skin side up in a 3-quart baking dish (9 × 13-inch or similar). Pour the reduced sauce over the chicken and cover the dish tightly with aluminum foil. Bake for 1 hour or until cooked through.

Move the chicken to a platter and spoon some of the sauce over the top. Garnish with the orange wheels. Serve the chicken with rice and pass the remaining sauce around the table.

You'll need a baking dish that holds all the pieces of chicken in a single layer—3 quarts is good.

Curried CHICKEN SALAD

EVIE • *This is another one of my mother's Spoleto party receipts. Guests would beg Mom to make the curried chicken salad at least two or three times during the two-week festival. I love the apples and raisins—they make it brighter and lighter than standard chicken salad and perfect for a warm summer day.*

STEPHEN • *One of the stranger things about our childhoods is that Evie and I never met as kids, even though we lived in a small town, our houses were one street apart, we had a raft of friends in common, and both of our mothers threw parties celebrating the visiting artists during the Spoleto Festival. (In fact, Evie and I met at one of these backyard parties, celebrating the world premiere of Philip Glass and Allen Ginsberg's* Hydrogen Jukebox.*) We both had a steady diet of cocktail party food, and finger sandwiches filled with this salad is one of my favorites.*

Side note: Having an international performing arts festival in your hometown is wonderfully educational in ways you don't expect. For instance: ballerinas are tiny, but they can really pack away the chow. I remember dance companies cleaning out a buffet like piranhas stripping the flesh off a cow.

Makes about 3 cups; 2 or 3 main-course servings or enough for 4 sandwiches

2 generous cups diced cooked chicken breast (about 1 pound; see the sidebar on page 61 for how to cook your own chicken)

½ cup mayonnaise, preferably Duke's

2 teaspoons curry powder

½ cup diced unpeeled apple (tart Granny Smiths are nice, or, if you prefer a sweeter apple, our favorites are Fujis)

1 good-sized stalk celery, trimmed and diced (about ½ cup)

⅓ cup golden raisins

¼ cup slivered almonds, toasted for a nuttier flavor

Salt and freshly ground pepper

Combine the chicken, mayonnaise, and curry powder in a medium bowl and stir until the curry is evenly mixed in. Add the apple, celery, raisins, and almonds, holding a few of the almonds back for sprinkling on top if you like. Mix well, then season with salt and pepper to taste.

Transfer the salad to a serving bowl and sprinkle the remaining almonds on top if you saved them. The chicken salad will keep in the refrigerator for up to 3 days.

NOTE

• Chicken salads—and curried chicken salads in particular—were made for tweaking. The recipe is a good starting point, but tailor it as you see fit. Maybe more raisins and fewer almonds? Less mayo and more curry? You're the boss.

Bunky Makes
SPATCHCOCKED
"YARDBIRD"

EVIE • *My sister, Madeleine, had the great good sense to marry a fabulous cook. My brother-in-law Bunky Wichmann is a natural-born teacher, and he personifies the adage that cooking is an act of love. Here he explains in supreme detail how to make the best grilled chicken in the world. Follow each step, and you will not only have a tasty chicken, but you just might feel inspired to share it with your friends and neighbors like Bunky does.*

STEPHEN • *I love my brother-in-law, but there is no denying that I am intimidated by his grill skills. He's kind, though, and every time he tastes one of my attempts at his recipes, he says, "I think you got away with it." I like trying to get away with this one, and you will, too. (Don't forget that grilling is hot work, so make sure you have a cold drink.)*

BUNKY • *A cooked chicken is often referred to as "yardbird" in the South because the chickens would often be found in a family's yard, whether that family lived on a farm or not. "Gospel chicken" is another colloquialism for this chicken in many African American communities, as it is often the meal of choice on Sundays—though more often fried rather than the way we are preparing our bird.*

First, you will want to start with a quality Bell & Evans or similar whole chicken that has been air-chilled. DO NOT waste your money buying a generic chicken that has been floating inside a plastic sealed bag in its own—and other—juices. These tend to come out with the consistency of a rubber tire. And do not worry so much about washing your bird. Cooking the chicken kills the bacteria. If you simply pat it dry with paper towels, that is fine. Just be sure to thoroughly wash any surfaces touched by the bird.

Spatchcocking a bird is straightforward: Remove the backbone with a large sharp knife or a cleaver (or a sturdy pair of kitchen shears). Remove any giblets that may be inside. Now take your knife and cut down the middle of the breastplate (sometimes called the keel bone)

continued —>

from the inside of the chicken. This will allow the bird to lay flat (almost) on your grill.

Season the bird on both sides with at least salt and pepper. I tend to like to use whatever spices are exciting me at the time: Bosari lemon pepper (or the simple lemon-pepper rub that follows), or "Slap Ya Momma" seasoning, which is fairly spicy. Don't worry about the spice level—a good bit gets lost in the cooking process. Refrigerate the seasoned bird, uncovered, for at least a few hours, or up to overnight, and take it out about 30 minutes before you start cooking. You'll get a crispier skin.

Prepare your grill while the bird is coming to room temp. I use a Big Green Egg, but any charcoal grill with an adjustable intake and flue will work. I use natural lump charcoal, which you can buy at most supermarkets. Just make sure NOT to use those pressed briquettes, which have all kinds of different materials to which we really don't want to have our food exposed.

You can either use indirect heat or simply grill the chicken right over the coals. Be careful with this second method, as it is easier to burn or char the bird if the heat gets too high.

Bring your grill to a nice hot temp of around 400°F. Make sure the actual grill surface is up to temperature. Oiling the grill surface will help keep the bird from sticking. I simply wipe it with an oil-damp paper towel or a silicone brush. I like to place my bird skin side down first for several minutes to get a little sear on the skin. Just let the bird sit there while the skin crisps up—moving it around before the skin crisps up will tear the skin. Flip the bird over and cook with the skin side up the rest of the time. Lower the grill temp to 300°F. As we have spatchcocked the bird, she will cook in almost half the time it takes for a whole bird. Cook until you reach an internal temp of no less than 160°F; check the temperature where the wing meets the breast and in the thickest part of the thighs, next to the bone. Grilling should only take about 30 to 40 minutes max. Do not overcook. Your chicken will come out with lovely moist meat and crispy skin. Let rest for about 10 minutes, cut, and serve. Your guest will be crazy about this yardbird of yours.

A VERY NON-BUNKY NOTE

• Spatchcocked yardbird can be cooked on a gas grill too. Heat the grill to 400°F and let the actual grill bars heat up for about 10 minutes before starting to grill. Proceed as above. The timing will be about the same. There is no comparison to charcoal, but what are you gonna do?

Lemon-Pepper Rub

Makes about ½ cup

3 lemons
⅓ cup coarse sea salt—Maldon is a great pick
2 tablespoons coarsely ground pepper

Wash the lemons and dry them very well. Line a small baking pan with
parchment or waxed paper. Grate the lemon zest coarsely right onto
the parchment—not with a Microplane-style zester, but one that is a little
coarser, like the finer one on the side of a box grater or a paddle-shaped
Parmesan cheese grater. Sprinkle the salt over the grated zest and toss
the two together. Let the lemon salt stand at room temperature until the
zest is dried out. (This process moves along quickly when it's less humid
or when the AC is running.)

When the lemon salt is ready, move it to a small bowl and stir in the
pepper. Store the rub in a spice jar for up to 2 months.

DUCK BREAST
with Fig-Orange Sauce

STEPHEN • *Those who have made the cauliflower puree (page 196) or the chickpea fries (page 52) will remember that at one point my doctor put me on a cholesterol-fighting diet. Cholesterol won. Part of his advice was, "Eat nothing with a hoof." If it swims or flies, I was allowed. Since steak was off the menu, I added duck to the regimen. To the letter of the law, but in clear violation of the spirit.*

EVIE • *Here is another way we use fig preserves from page 280 . . . Actually, I usually skip the duck breast, but to be honest, I will spoon the delicious sauce onto a slice of bread when no one is looking. Shhh!*

Makes 2 servings

2 boneless duck breasts (about 1 pound)

Salt and freshly ground pepper

Juice of 1 orange

½ cup fig preserves, homemade (page 280) or store-bought

1 tablespoon soy sauce

1 tablespoon honey

Thin strips of orange zest (optional)

Turn the duck breasts skin side down on a cutting board and trim off any skin/fat that pokes out past the meat. Flip them over and score the skin in a crosshatch pattern using a very sharp knife, being careful not to cut all the way through the fat layer to the meat. Pat the breasts dry and salt and pepper them generously.

Lay the breasts skin side down in a cold skillet large enough to hold them comfortably and set over medium heat. As the temperature comes up, the fat under the skin will render out through the scoring. Pour it off as you go, but save it to use in other recipes, like the Smashed Potatoes on page 195, as well as to finish the sauce here.

The duck will do most of the cooking on the skin side. Once the skin is deep gold and crisp, turn the duck over. Cook until the internal temperature reaches 125°F in the thickest part of the breast—this will give you medium-rare duck. Remove it from the pan and let rest, covered, for about 8 minutes.

While the duck rests, make the sauce: Pour off all the fat from the pan. Deglaze the pan with the orange juice, stirring to lift the delicious duck flavors. Add the fig preserves (I've used plum preserves or marmalade as well), soy sauce, and honey and simmer until the sauce is reduced by a quarter. Stir in a tablespoon of the reserved duck fat and the orange zest, if using.

Cut the duck across the grain, at an angle, into ½-inch-thick slices. Fan the slices out on two plates, drizzle liberally with the sauce, and serve. The duck is so rich and meaty, you'd swear it had a hoof.

CHICKEN THIGHS
with Mustard-Mushroom Sauce

EVIE • *We are huge fans of Ina Garten and have many of her cookbooks. I have made her chicken thighs with mustard sauce so many times that my family finally begged me to change it up a bit. (I sometimes get into a phase and make the same thing over and over again!) So we tweaked it a little bit and added the mushrooms. It is equally as delicious and gives you an added bonus of sneaking an extra vegetable into the meal as well!*

STEPHEN • *Not to be "that guy," but I am that guy—mushrooms are not vegetables. They are fungus. Because I took the time to point that out, I'm sure Evie is thinking, "You are fungus." That said, Evie is right, we love Ina and her recipes, and this is one we make often. The addition of the mushrooms gives this something of a stroganoff quality, so serving it over a bed of egg noodles feels just about right.*

Makes 4 servings

Olive oil

8 bone-in, skin-on chicken thighs (about 2¼ pounds)

Salt and freshly ground pepper

½ pound cremini or button mushrooms, trimmed and thinly sliced (about 2 cups)

1 medium yellow onion, thinly sliced (about 2 cups)

¼ cup dry white wine

¾ cup sour cream or full-fat Greek yogurt

¼ cup chicken broth, homemade or store-bought

1 tablespoon Dijon mustard

2 teaspoons whole-grain mustard

1 teaspoon salt, or as needed

2 tablespoons chopped fresh flat-leaf parsley

You'll need a mighty big pan to hold all 8 chicken thighs—at least 14 inches measured across the bottom. If you don't have a pan of that size, cook the chicken in two pans, dividing all the ingredients evenly between the pans.

Pour enough olive oil into a large cast-iron or other heavy skillet to coat the bottom and heat over medium heat until rippling. Meanwhile, season the thighs on both sides with salt and pepper. When the oil is hot, slip in the thighs skin side down and cook until the skin is well browned, about 10 minutes.

Move the thighs to a plate. Add the mushrooms and onion to the pan and stir to coat with the rendered chicken fat. Cook for a few minutes. Place the thighs back in the pan, on top of the mushrooms and onion. Cook until the thickest part of a thigh near the bone is no longer pink (at least 165°F on an instant-read thermometer).

Move the chicken to a plate, leaving the mushrooms and onion in the pan. If the vegetables are watery and/or not quite brown, stir until the liquid has boiled off and the vegetables are browned. Deglaze the pan with the wine, stirring to release the brown bits that have stuck to the bottom. Stir in the sour cream, chicken broth, Dijon and grainy mustards, and salt. Cook, stirring, until everything is blended and the sauce is bubbling.

Tuck the chicken into the sauce, skin side up, and simmer for a minute or two. Taste the sauce and add salt if you like. Sprinkle the parsley over everything and serve right from the pan. We like to serve it over noodles.

SALT-AND-PEPPER WINGS

STEPHEN • *These are my attempt to re-create the fantastic salt-and-pepper wings from a local NYC kitchen called La Poulette. I order them when I need something to pick up my spirits. They are very simple to make, and as my version is baked, not fried, I tell myself they are healthy.*

EVIE • *There are several things that Stephen turns to for comfort.* Lord of the Rings *is, of course, top of the list, and then old episodes of* Veep, *but these delicious yet easy chicken wings also are a go-to for calming the brain and restoring the spirit.*

Makes 6 appetizer servings

2 pounds chicken wings (the kind that are already cut into "half-wings")

2 teaspoons salt

1 teaspoon baking powder

Vegetable oil for the wire rack

2 teaspoons finely ground pepper

> You'll need a wire rack to get the skin nice and crisp. An ordinary cooling rack will work beautifully.

Wash the wings and pat them as dry as possible. Place them on a paper towel–lined plate and refrigerate, uncovered, for an hour or two. The drier the skin, the crispier the wings will cook up.

Heat the oven to 250°F with a rack in the center position. While that's happening, toss the wings in a mixture of 1 teaspoon of the salt and the baking powder. Use your hands to make sure the mixture is rubbed over all the wings. Lightly oil a cooling rack and set it over a baking sheet. Lay the wings out on it, with enough room between them for air to circulate.

Bake for 30 minutes. (The low oven temp helps with the skin drying/crisping.) Turn the oven up to 425°F and continue baking until the skin is browned and crisp, about 45 minutes. You may want to flip the wings for the last 15 minutes to even out the browning.

Remove the wings to a bowl and toss with the remaining 1 teaspoon salt and the pepper. Enjoy the fatty, salty, crispy, happy.

NOTE

• If you want a wing dip, try the Mango-Cilantro Sauce (page 86) or the Green Goddess Dip (page 40).

LIME-MEZCAL WINGS

STEPHEN • *These wings are cooked the same way as the Salt-and-Pepper Wings on page 107, but they are marinated before and sauced after. This recipe came about because I had a lot of Key limes that were at a "use it or lose it" stage and a new bottle of Dos Hombres mezcal given to me by the dos hombres themselves, Aaron Paul and Bryan Cranston. What do you know? It worked. Yeah, science!*

EVIE • *I am not sure if it is the mezcal or Key limes, but these are so so good and make the kitchen smell so delicious that it almost makes me want to eat chicken again.*

*
pictured
with Salt-
and-Pepper
Wings on
page 106

Makes 6 appetizer servings

½ cup fresh lime juice (from Key limes if possible!)

¼ cup Dos Hombres or other good-quality mezcal

¼ cup extra-virgin olive oil

4 cloves garlic, crushed

2 tablespoons Auggie's Fennel-Bourbon Candied Hot Peppers (page 27), finely chopped, or 2 teaspoons sugar plus 1 teaspoon red pepper flakes

2 teaspoons salt

2 pounds chicken wings (the kind already cut into "half-wings")

1 teaspoon fine salt

1 teaspoon baking powder

2 tablespoons honey

Stir the lime juice, mezcal, olive oil, garlic, peppers, and salt together in a large bowl. Add the wings and toss well, then remove the wings and mezcal mixture to a container that suits you: I like the convenience and utility of a gallon zip-lock bag, but the environmental cost of single-use plastic is not lost on me. So use a better container, you better person reading this.

Marinate the wings in the fridge for, oh, maybe 4 hours? I can never judge. The lime juice and mezcal mix is pretty potent, but I don't think that overnight would hurt ya.

Take the wings out of the bag, drain them well, and retain the marinade—this will be boiled down into the sauce, if you don't want to squeeze a lot more limes.

Pat the wings as dry as possible. Place them on a paper towel–lined plate and refrigerate, uncovered, for an hour or two. The drier the skin, the crispier the wings will cook up.

Heat the oven to 250°F with a rack in the center position. While that's happening, toss the wings in a mixture of fine salt and baking powder. Use your hands to make sure the mixture is rubbed over all the wings. Lightly oil a cooling rack and set it over a baking sheet. Lay the wings out on it, with enough room between them for air to circulate.

Bake for 30 minutes. (The low oven temp helps with the skin drying/crisping.) Turn the oven up to 425°F and continue baking until the skin is browned and crisp, about 45 minutes. You may want to flip the wings for the last 15 minutes to even out the browning.

While the wings are baking, make the sauce: Strain the marinade into a saucepan, bring to a low simmer, and simmer for 5 minutes. Add the honey and bring the sauce to a foaming boil, then kill the heat. The sauce should be golden and fragrant and approximately the consistency of maple syrup; if it is not, boil for a minute or two more.

When the wings are done, put them in a bowl, pour the lime-mezcal sauce over them, and toss until they are coated. Serve the crispy, tart, and sweet wings.

Whole Roasted
BUTTERMILK CHICKEN

STEPHEN • *I love the look and smell of a roasted chicken. It has a mid-century Norman Rockwell, family-at-table quality that I find more comforting the older I get . . . which I keep getting. Plus, the leftovers sandwiches alone are worth the effort, which admittedly is pretty low.*

For whatever reason, my buttermilk brining has always resulted in some uneven browning of the skin. Maybe I don't get enough of the buttermilk off. I have had some success rubbing the whole bird with a stick of butter 15 minutes before it's done. Not only does this help, but it's butter!

EVIE • *Nothing says family dinner time more to me than the smell of a roast chicken. When the children were younger, I would serve roast chicken at least once a week. I didn't know about this delicious buttermilk receipt back then, though (and frankly I am not sure I would have planned ahead well enough to marinate it overnight), but I am sure the kids would have been really impressed with me if I had. This chicken is so so moist you won't believe it, and your family will be so impressed with you.*

continued —→

Makes 4 servings

Salt

One 3- to 4-pound roasting chicken

1 quart buttermilk

2 tablespoon chopped fresh rosemary

1 tablespoon fresh thyme leaves

1 teaspoon garlic powder

1 lemon

1 medium onion

> You'll need a roasting rack for the chicken, but a sturdy cooling rack will do in a pinch.

Salt the chicken liberally inside and out, then set aside while you mix together the buttermilk, rosemary, thyme, and garlic powder in a small bowl. (You can use dried thyme, but I don't recommend dried rosemary, unless you like getting stabbed in the mouth by pine needles.)

Place the chicken in a gallon zip-lock bag and pour in the buttermilk mixture. Squeeze out the extra air and seal the bag. Refrigerate for 12 to 24 hours, turning the chicken several times as it sits.

Take the chicken out of the bag and squeegee off the excess buttermilk with your fingers, inside and out. (You don't have to wash it off.) Quarter the lemon and the (peeled) onion and stuff the pieces into the chicken cavity. Let the chicken come to room temp while you heat the oven to 425°F.

Place the chicken on a roasting rack set in a baking pan and cook for 20 minutes. Turn the pan around for even cooking and reduce the heat to 375°F. Cook for another 30 minutes, or until the internal temperature in the thickest part of a thigh is 165°F. Remove the chicken from the oven and let rest for 15 minutes, lightly covered in foil.

If you're the person who carves the turkey on Thanksgiving, go ahead and carve the chicken to serve it. If not, the easiest way to serve a whole roasted chicken is to cut it up: Use sturdy kitchen shears to cut down along both sides of the backbone to remove it. Cut (or snip) the bird in half through the breastbone and then cut each half into leg and breast pieces.

CHRISTMAS BEEF WELLINGTON
116

PORT WINE REDUCTION
123

STEAK AU POIVRE
125

LAMB BOLOGNESE SAUCE
128

BILL'S BEER BRISKET
130

TERIYAKI PORK TENDERLOIN
133

SMOKED BOURBON–BROWN SUGAR
PORK BELLY SLIDERS WITH PICKLED SLAW
134

QUICK-PICKLED APPLE-ONION SLAW
137

BUNKY MAKES PULLED PORK
139

MEAT

"Meat" is a vague word. It can mean a lot of things. Chicken is meat, but "meat" is not chicken. For our purposes, meat comes from anything with a hoof. So, everything I'm not supposed to have. (Note to self: tear out this chapter in my doctor's copy.)

Evie and I have different relationships to meat. I like it, especially slow-smoked barbeque pork. It's meat candy. Evie can take it or leave it, and mostly she leaves it.

But I do remember The Lost Burger. By the time Evie was pregnant with our first child, I had known her for five years, and, in that time, I had never seen her take so much as a bite of red meat. Never made a fuss, just didn't care for it. But about a month before Maddie was born, I made myself a thick, juicy cheeseburger with grilled onions. As I sat down to eat it, Evie looked over and said, "I feel like I want a bite of that." I said, "Really? But . . ." "I know, I just feel like I want to try one bite." I never saw it again. So, Dads-to-Be, remember: burgers for the third trimester and rhubarb crisp (see page 224) for postpartum recovery. • STEPHEN

Christmas
BEEF
WELLINGTON

EVIE • *We have always been a turkey family. Roast turkey for Thanksgiving and roast turkey for Christmas. But one Christmas a few years ago, my mother said she really wanted to have beef Wellington. She might as well have said she wanted escargots flown in from Paris. My sister and I looked at her with huge eyes and said, "How do you make that?" But Stephen said he would give it a try, and he made her the most delicious beef Wellington. She adored it and he made it for her every Christmas after that until she died. He still makes it at Christmas, and we all love it, because it reminds us of Mom. Thank you, honey, for making my mother's Christmas dinner so special for so many years.*

continued $\longrightarrow$

THE BEEF

1 fully trimmed beef tenderloin
(about 4 pounds)

2 tablespoons olive oil

THE MUSHROOM SPREAD (AKA DUXELLES)

3 tablespoons butter

3 small shallots, minced

1 pound button mushrooms,
wiped clean, trimmed, and
sliced

Salt and freshly ground
pepper

THE ASSEMBLY

30 slices prosciutto (about
½ pound; ask that the
prosciutto be sliced a tiny
bit thicker than usual)

Salt and freshly ground
pepper

3 tablespoons Dijon mustard,
or as needed

One 17.3-ounce box frozen
puff pastry (2 sheets)

1 egg, well beaten with
1 tablespoon water,
for egg wash

Port Wine Reduction (recipe
follows)

> The prosciutto-wrapped
> beef tenderloin is best
> prepared the night before,
> as it will need to chill
> thoroughly before you wrap
> it in the pastry. Also, you'll
> absolutely want an instant-
> read thermometer for this.

Prep and sear the beef: Cut the tenderloin crosswise in half. Tuck the "tail" of the tenderloin underneath and tie with several lengths of kitchen twine. You should now have 2 pieces of tenderloin of approximately the same thickness.

Heat the olive oil in a large, heavy skillet over medium-high heat. Sear the pieces of tenderloin one at a time, until very well browned on all sides, including the ends; remove the first piece once it is seared, and add some fresh oil before searing the second piece. Let the beef cool while you continue your prep.

Make the mushroom spread (duxelles): Heat the butter in a large sauté pan over medium heat until foaming. Stir in the shallots and cook until wilted, about 3 minutes. Stir in the mushrooms and cook until the liquid the mushrooms give off has evaporated and the mushrooms are browned, about 12 minutes. Scrape the mix into a food processor and pulse to a spreadable consistency. Scrape into a bowl, season with salt and pepper, and set aside to cool.

Assemble the Wellingtons: Tear off two pieces of plastic wrap that are about 2 inches longer than the tenderloin piece you're starting with. Overlap the wrap to make a large square. Shingle half the prosciutto slices over the center of the plastic wrap. The area you cover with prosciutto should be a little longer than the tenderloin (on both ends) and wide enough to completely wrap around the tenderloin. Spread half the mushroom duxelles over the prosciutto. Season the cooled beef generously with salt and pepper and smear it with enough Dijon mustard to coat it lightly. Center the beef over the prosciutto and roll up, completely enclosing the beef. Twist the ends of the plastic like the wrapper on a hard candy and tuck under the beef roll. Repeat this process with the other piece of tenderloin and the remaining prosciutto and duxelles. Refrigerate the wrapped beef overnight.

One hour before roasting, remove the tenderloin rolls from the fridge and move the puff pastry from the freezer to the counter, so it will be defrosted when it comes time to wrap the tenderloins.

Heat the oven to 450°F with a rack in the center position. Roll out one sheet of puff pastry on a lightly floured countertop to a rectangle about 1½ inches longer than the first beef-prosciutto roll and wide enough to overlap slightly when wrapped around it. Bring the sides of the pastry up to meet over the tenderloin and

continued ⟶

pinch them together to seal. Turn the roll seam side down. Trim some of the pastry from the ends if necessary, so there is just enough to tuck the ends underneath and make a compact roll with nice smooth ends; refrigerate the dough trimmings. Using the tip of a paring knife, make 1½-inch slits, about 1 inch apart, down the top. Carefully move the Wellington to a baking sheet large enough to hold both finished Wellingtons. Repeat with the second piece of tenderloin and the remaining pastry.

Brush the Wellingtons well with the egg wash. Press the scraps of dough together, roll them out, and use cutters to make decorative shapes. (Leaf shapes are nice.) Decorate the tops of the Wellingtons with these cutouts and brush again with egg.

Roast the Wellingtons for 20 minutes. Rotate the baking pan and continue roasting until the beef is 125°F at the center of the thickest point, about 15 additional minutes. You really need a thermometer for this one! Remove the beef and let stand for 20 minutes before serving.

To serve: Carve the Wellingtons into 1-inch-thick slices (you can use the slits you cut on top as a rough guide). Carefully lift the slices onto plates and spoon a little of the port wine sauce over and around each one.

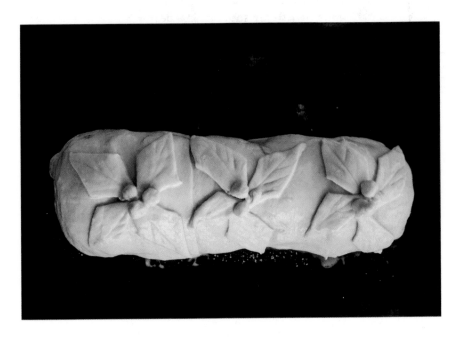

PORT WINE
Reduction

STEPHEN • *I saw a recipe like this in an in-flight magazine as a sidebar to skillet-fried salmon and tore it out. For years, I would fish out the folded page that was tucked in the corner of the kitchen behind the stand mixer until one day, due to some fit of orderliness, it was gone. I can't find the old recipe online, so I have been making it from memory for about the last fifteen years. The rich, sweet, and tart sauce goes well on salmon, steak, or chicken, or rubbed on your gums.*

EVIE • *"Fit of orderliness"?—shots fired!! I challenge anyone to keep a folded piece of paper in a corner of their kitchen for years. We all know that is what old cookbooks are for . . . to store new recipes that have been torn out of magazines! Did you look in* The Joy of Cooking, *hon?*

Makes about 1½ cups

1 tablespoon extra-virgin
olive oil

1 large shallot, minced

1 apple, cored and roughly
chopped

1 medium carrot, peeled and
roughly chopped

1 bottle (750 ml) dry red wine

6 to 8 sprigs thyme, tied in
a small bouquet with kitchen
string

1 cup tawny port wine

1 cup beef or chicken broth,
homemade or store-bought

4 tablespoons (½ stick)
unsalted butter,
cut into 4 pieces

Salt and freshly ground
pepper

Heat the olive oil in a 2-quart saucepan over medium heat. Stir in the shallot, and once it takes on some color, 5 to 6 minutes, add the apple and carrot. Stir until the apple starts releasing some liquid and the carrot is beginning to soften. Pour in the full bottle of red wine, add the thyme bouquet, bring to a simmer, and simmer until the wine has reduced by half. Strain the mixture and return to the clean pan.

Add the port wine and stock, bring to a slow boil, and boil until the liquid has reduced by half again. Remove the sauce from the heat and whisk in the butter piece by piece. Season with salt and pepper to taste and serve.

STEAK
au Poivre

EVIE • *One of our family traditions is that on your birthday you get to pick what we eat for dinner. When the kids were younger, by far the most frequent request was steak and fries. I would always add a veggie or salad, but oddly, that was never part of the request!*

STEPHEN • *Steak au poivre is my brother Ed's specialty. It's always great fun when he and his wife, Kitty (she of Green Goddess fame; see page 40), visit. While Kitty appears to live on Diet Coke, crispy bacon, and Pinot Grigio, they both appreciate an extended cocktail hour that often ends with Ed searing meat and holding forth on any number of subjects, the more obscure the better. We Colbert siblings are all champion talkers who love the wise and mellifluous sound of our own voices.*

WHY HANGER STEAK?

Hanger steak is a tender, often overlooked, cut of meat that is perfect for this dish because of its robust flavor. This cut can be hard to find—restaurants snatch it up to use as the "steak" part of a steak frites. If you do score a hanger steak, be sure to slice it against the grain, as you would any steak, after cooking. If you can't find hanger steak, a New York strip steak works beautifully here.

continued →

Makes 2 servings

1 hanger steak (about ¾ pound; see the sidebar)

2 tablespoons dried green peppercorns

1 to 1½ teaspoons coarsely ground pepper

Salt

2 tablespoons brandy

2 tablespoons unsalted butter

1 tablespoon olive oil

¼ cup beef broth, homemade or store-bought

¼ cup heavy cream, at room temperature

Using a meat mallet, lightly pound the steak to an even thickness. Rub the green and black pepper into both sides of the steak and then season generously with salt. Let stand at room temperature for an hour, give or take 10 minutes.

While the beef is standing, measure the brandy into a small cup or bowl. (It is always safer to add an alcoholic ingredient to a hot pan from a small container than from the original bottle.)

Heat the oven to 350°F. Add the butter and oil to a heavy skillet over medium-high heat. (If you're sure you won't set off the smoke alarm and your ventilation can handle it, go ahead and use high heat. Just know you'll have to move fast.) The butter will foam and then the foamy bits will start to turn brown. Wait until this happens to add the steak to the pan, then sear it on both sides for about 2 minutes each to get a nice dark golden crust.

Remove the pan from the heat, put the steak on a small baking sheet, and put it in the oven. Cook the steak until done to your liking. Best bet: Use an instant-read thermometer (see page 90). Cook to 120°F for rare steak, 130°F for medium-rare.

While the steak is in the oven, return the pan to the heat and carefully add the brandy to it. The brandy will almost certainly flame up, so make sure to stand back from the pan. Use a wooden spoon to scrape up all the delicious little bits stuck to the bottom. The brandy will evaporate quickly—before the pan is dry, add the beef broth and heavy cream. Reduce the heat to low and cook the pan sauce until reduced by about one-third. Remove the pan from the heat and keep the sauce warm.

When the steak is done, remove it to a carving board, cover it loosely with aluminum foil, and let it rest for at least 10 minutes before slicing. Slice the steak on a slight angle against the grain. Overlap the slices on a platter or plates, pour the pepper sauce over them, and dig in.

Lamb
BOLOGNESE SAUCE

EVIE • *Our friend Emily Lazar Alter gave us this receipt. The Bolognese is so delicious that the pasta is really just an afterthought. The sauce could be eaten alone as a stew. Don't be put off by the amounts (yes, that is an entire bottle of red wine in there). It makes a lot.*

STEPHEN • *Emily used to give us a two-quart jar of this sauce at Christmastime, but we couldn't wait all year for the next batch, so she confided the recipe, and we're blabbing it here. I agree with Evie that it's good enough to be eaten as a stew—or to be eaten with a spoon straight out of the jar, as I have caught Evie doing on more than one occasion. (VERY selective vegan.)*

**Makes about 10 cups
(2½ to 3 cups is enough to
sauce 1 pound of pasta—
refrigerate or freeze the rest!)**

⅓ pound unsmoked bacon,
cut into medium dice
(about 1 lightly packed cup)

2 tablespoons unsalted butter

2 tablespoons extra-virgin
olive oil

1½ cups finely chopped yellow
onions (about 2 small onions)

¾ cup finely chopped celery
(about 2 medium stalks)

¾ cup finely chopped carrots
(about 2 small carrots)

Salt and freshly ground
pepper

2 cloves garlic, minced

1 pound ground lamb

1⅓ cups tomato paste

1½ cups whole milk

1 bottle (750 ml) dry red wine

One 28-ounce can whole
tomatoes, drained of their
juices and squished to small
pieces with your hands
(about 2⅔ cups)

4 cups beef broth, homemade
or store-bought

1 pound rotini, pappardelle,
or other "big" pasta

Grated Parmesan or
Pecorino Romano

Put the bacon in a 4- to 5-quart Dutch oven or other heavy, wide pot and set over medium heat. Cook, stirring, until lightly browned, about 5 minutes. Scoop the bacon out with a slotted spoon, leaving the drippings in the pot, and set aside.

Add the butter and olive oil to the pot and continue to cook over medium heat. When the butter is foaming, stir in the onions, celery, and carrots and season with salt and pepper. Sauté, stirring frequently, until the vegetables soften.

Add the garlic and sauté for a minute, then add the lamb. Season again with salt and pepper. Cook, stirring occasionally, until the lamb is thoroughly browned, about 10 minutes. Add the tomato paste along with the bacon and cook for 5 minutes, stirring occasionally.

Add the milk and simmer until the milk is absorbed, 10 to 15 minutes. Add the wine and cook over low heat until most of the liquid is absorbed. This can take up to 30 minutes.

Stir in the tomatoes and broth, bring to a simmer, and cook over low heat until the sauce is reduced and "comes together," about 3 hours. Skim the fat off the surface and remove from the heat. Set aside 3 cups of sauce for the pasta and refrigerate or freeze the rest. The sauce can be refrigerated for up to 1 week or frozen for up to 6 months.

To serve with pasta: Bring a large pot of salted water to a boil. Add the pasta and cook, stirring occasionally, until the pasta is al dente. (A good rule of thumb for al dente pasta is to cook for 1 to 2 minutes less than suggested on the package.) Reserve a cup of the pasta cooking water. Drain the pasta, return it to the pot, and stir in enough sauce to liberally coat it. Add a little of the reserved water to "set up" a thin sauce or loosen a thick sauce—it works both ways!—and bring to a simmer

Serve immediately, topped with grated cheese.

Bill's
BEER BRISKET

EVIE • *This is one of those dishes that you need to plan ahead to make, not only because it takes a long time, but because while it is cooking, your house will smell so divine that everyone will suddenly want to stay for dinner. Which is no problem, because you can feed an army of hungry friends (or a smaller army of hungry teenagers) with this delicious dish.*

STEPHEN • *This is an easy recipe that tastes and smells like the 1970s to me. We had it a lot, especially for big get-togethers. Many members of my family claim this one. My sister Mary says it's hers, Evie and I found the recipe in my mom's slim card catalogue, and my sister-in-law Susan sent it to us as one of my late brother Bill's recipes. Mary's probably right, but it makes me happy to see Bill's name in this book, so he gets the honors.*

Makes at least 12 servings

1 large yellow onion, sliced

1 brisket (about 4 pounds; see Notes)

Garlic salt

One 12-ounce can beer (not light beer)

½ cup packed brown sugar

½ bottle chili sauce

Heat the oven to 350°F with a rack in the center position. Line a 13 × 9-inch inch baking pan with aluminum foil. Spray the foil lightly with cooking spray.

Spread out the sliced onion in the lined pan. Place the brisket on top and season well with garlic salt. (Start with a teaspoon and go from there.) Whisk the beer, brown sugar, and chili sauce in a medium bowl until blended. Pour over the brisket.

Cover the brisket pan with more foil, making sure there is a nice tight seal all the way around the pan. Bake until the brisket is very tender, 3 to 4 hours. Don't test for doneness until at least 2½ hours into the cooking—if the brisket isn't done, tightly reseal the foil all around the pan using oven mitts. When the brisket is tender, remove it from the oven and let it sit in the covered baking pan for at least 30 minutes.

Transfer the brisket to a carving board and carve it into slices against the grain. Overlap the slices on a platter and spoon some of the sauce and onions over them.

NOTES

• There are all kinds of brisket cuts out there, but they can be broken down into two main types: "the flat" and "the point." The flat is, well, flat and the point is thicker and rounder. The flat is what you will almost always find at the supermarket. It has a nice layer of fat over the meat, which helps keep the brisket moist during cooking. The flat is also easier to carve, as the grain is very easy to identify.

• The brisket can be cooked the day before and refrigerated. Carve the chilled brisket into thickish slices and arrange them overlapping in the same pan they were cooked in. To serve, cover the pan with aluminum foil and heat the slices in a 350°F oven for about 30 minutes.

• For a thicker, heartier sauce, spoon the juices into a saucepan, bring to a boil, and reduce until thickened.

Teriyaki
PORK TENDERLOIN

EVIE • *A pork tenderloin is one of those quick and easy go-to meals. This marinade is sweet and wonderful, and I found it was an excellent way to get my children to eat pork when they were young. And if you don't have time to marinate the pork, you can brush on a little sauce and pop it in the oven.*

STEPHEN • *This sweet, salty recipe also makes excellent leftovers. I know because this recipe had its heyday when the kids were younger, and I was at my professional busiest. I'm sorry to say I missed quite a few of these pork loins . . . and a few bedtimes. Great! Now I'm crying.*

Makes 4 servings

⅓ cup soy sauce

⅓ cup orange juice

3 tablespoons light brown sugar

1 tablespoon vegetable oil, plus more for the baking pan

1 tablespoon minced fresh ginger

2 cloves garlic, minced

1½ teaspoons sesame oil

1 pork tenderloin (about 1½ pounds)

2 to 3 green onions, trimmed and thinly sliced, for garnish

3 tablespoons toasted sesame seeds, for garnish

Combine the soy sauce, orange juice, brown sugar, vegetable oil, ginger, garlic, and sesame oil in a small saucepan and bring to a boil, then reduce the heat to medium-low and boil gently until the marinade just starts to get syrupy (you'll have about ⅔ cup). Let cool completely.

Put the tenderloin in a 1-gallon resealable plastic bag. Pour in half the cooled marinade—you can eyeball it—and squish it around until the tenderloin is coated. Set the rest of the marinade aside for later. Refrigerate the pork for at least 30 minutes, and up to 4 hours.

Heat the oven to 450°F with a rack in the lowest position. Line a baking sheet large enough to hold the tenderloin with aluminum foil. Coat the foil with vegetable oil. Add the tenderloin and cook until an instant-read thermometer inserted into the thickest part of the tenderloin reads 145°F (the pork will continue to cook out of the oven), 17 to 20 minutes. Remove from the oven, cover loosely with aluminum foil, and let rest for at least 10 minutes before carving.

Cut the tenderloin into ½-inch-thick slices and arrange on a platter or individual plates. Drizzle with the remaining marinade. Garnish with the green onions and sesame seeds.

Smoked BOURBON–BROWN SUGAR PORK BELLY SLIDERS *with Pickled Slaw*

STEPHEN • *When we go to our farmers' market, or a good butcher shop, I like getting a cut of meat that you don't often see at the grocery store, though this one is a cut that we often see in a processed form. Pork belly is the bacon cut—a cap of fat with layers of richly marbled meat. Time is your friend here, to marinate, to render the fat, and to crisp the top. Every slice will be a rich serving, so you'll want to pair this with something crisp and acidic—in this case, a quick-pickled apple and onion slaw, which I first made when I realized I had forgotten to get cabbage and had only apple cider vinegar. I was worried, but it worked! I hope everything works out for you.*

These smoked pork belly sliders are fatty, sweet, and crispy—and you will eat more than you planned to.

EVIE • *The smoking for this photo took Stephen 9 hours and 15 minutes, but he didn't seem to mind all that grill time, as long as he had a cool drink in his hand. While I don't eat pork, I have been assured by our friends that these pork belly sliders are incredible, and the pickled slaw adds just the right amount of zippy tang. I do eat slaw.*

continued →

A 3-pound cut of pork belly, skin removed

1 cup packed brown sugar

½ cup salt

½ cup bourbon, or enough to make a thick slurry with the sugar and salt

1 tablespoon garlic powder

1 tablespoon ground ginger

¼ cup maple syrup

¼ cup warm water

2 tablespoons soy sauce

Quick-Pickled Apple-Onion Slaw (recipe follows)

Soft slider rolls (I like King's Hawaiian)

You'll need a charcoal smoker and chunks of applewood or cherrywood for said smoker. Also, you might want to call around to track down pork belly in one large piece.

tip—If managing flare-ups is more than you want to deal with, you can crisp the top in the oven set on broil. Keep that vent on high, and don't walk away!

Score the fat cap of the pork in a 2-inch diamond pattern and put the belly in a large resealable plastic bag. Mix the brown sugar, salt, bourbon, garlic, and ginger together and pour over the pork belly. Press out the air before sealing the bag, then refrigerate the pork for at least 24 hours, and up to 2 days.

Remove the pork from the marinade, rinse, and pat dry. Get your smoker set up for indirect heat and light the coals. While the coals are heating up, soak some applewood or cherrywood chunks in water. Combine the maple syrup, water, and soy sauce in a spray bottle and shake well to mix.

When the coals are ready, nestle the wood chips into them. Cook the pork, fat cap up, over indirect heat at 250°F. The timing can vary widely depending on the size of the cut and size of the grill. The key is to cook the pork belly until you reach an internal temperature of 190°F. During the last hour, spray the pork every 15 minutes with the maple syrup mixture. When the pork is ready, take it off the grill grate and set it aside while you spread out the coals and bring them to high heat.

Return the pork, fat side down, to the high heat and keep a spray bottle of water handy to kill the flames that will inevitably flare up from the dripping fat. After about a minute, remove the pork. The goal is a crisp char, not blackening. Wrap the meat in foil and set aside for 15 minutes.

Make the sliders: After the pork has rested, cut the slab into 2-inch-wide strips, then cut the strips into ½-inch-wide slices. I like to build my slider with a slice of the pork, topped with the quick-pickled slaw and a drizzle of a sweet barbeque sauce.

Quick-Pickled Apple-Onion Slaw

Makes about 2 cups

1 cup apple cider vinegar
⅓ cup packed light brown sugar
1 tablespoon salt
1 cup ice cubes
1 medium onion
1 Honey Crisp apple (or another similarly sweet/crisp combo)

Combine the vinegar, brown sugar, and salt in a saucepan and bring to a simmer over medium heat. Simmer, stirring, until the sugar is dissolved. Then add the ice. This will make the liquid usable immediately. It is a quick pickle, after all. Remove from the heat.

Slice the onion very thin. Core the apple, cut it into thin slices, then cut the slices into short matchsticks. I like to keep the skin on for extra crunch.

Put the apple and onion in a glass jar or bowl and cover with the pickling liquid. If you do this right after the pork goes on, the slaw will be ready long before the pork comes off the grill. Pour off the liquid before serving.

Bunky Makes
PULLED PORK

STEPHEN • *Bunky is the son of a son of a sailor, and the saltiest dog I know. His grandfather was the last keeper of the Cape Romain Light, and his father was born in that lighthouse. A lover of wooden boats, good beer, and barbequed meats, Bunky is easy company and a good man that I am so lucky to have as a friend, as family, and as a meat mentor. Heed his smoky wisdom, reader.*

BUNKY • *Pulled pork is one of the great things about living in the South: everyone has their own recipe. There are almost infinite ways to prepare it right and only a few ways to do it wrong.*

First, select your meat from a good butcher. The cut I am using in this recipe is the top of the pork shoulder, also known as a Boston butt, though almost everything still applies if you decide to do a full shoulder.

I cook—or smoke—my BBQ in a Big Green Egg, but any reasonably good charcoal grill will do as long as there is a way to adjust the air flow intake at the bottom and the top in order to regulate the temp. I only use natural lump charcoal, as it burns the cleanest and has no chemicals or additives like the "briquets" you can buy. There are several really good brands on the market that can be procured at most supermarkets or specialty shops. I like the Cowboy brand or the Big Green Egg brand, as the chunks are often larger and thus burn longer. You will want to prep your meat the day before, and have as much fuel in your firebox as you can fit, as it will need to burn for as long as 8 hours.

continued →

Makes 12 servings

One 7- to 9-pound pork shoulder roast (Boston butt)

THE RUB

½ cup packed brown sugar

1 teaspoon mustard powder

1 tablespoon kosher salt

1 tablespoon freshly ground pepper

2 tablespoons smoked paprika

1 tablespoon onion powder

1 tablespoon garlic powder

1 teaspoon cayenne pepper

From prep to serving, this is a 24-hour recipe, including 8 hours of smoking.

Start preparing the pork 24 hours or so before you are planning to cook/smoke it, remembering that the smoking process will take 6 to 8 hours. Begin by cutting the butt into rectangular chunks—around 6 by 4 by 4 inches or so. Try to cut along the natural lines of the shoulder if possible. Next, you want to apply your rub, mixed from the dry ingredients. Apply this generously and cover all sides. Let the pork sit in the fridge, covered, overnight at least. Your fridge will smell wonderful in the morning.

Get your fire going and make sure to load the cooker up with fuel. You will likely want to add some wood chips to smoke the meat. I tend to like hickory, while others like mesquite, maple, or cherry. If possible, use indirect heat, as you are really smoking more than cooking. Bring your temp to a steady 300°F. Place your pork "bricks" fat side up on the grill so they do not touch each other. The smoke needs to be able to engulf the meat on all sides. The temp will naturally drop back when you put the pork in the cooker/smoker. Dial down the smoker to 250°F and cook/smoke for approximately 6 to 8 hours. The pork is done when the internal temp is 160°F.

Remove the pork and let it rest a bit before you start to pull the meat apart. You can use your gloved hands along with bear claw meat shredders, which really help in the process. Discard any fatty pieces or any bone that is left. Some people like to chop their pork down into small bits; others leave it in longer, stringy pieces.

SEA BASS IN
WHITE WINE BUTTER
150

PANFRIED SPOT TAIL BASS
152

FLOUNDER STUFFED WITH
DEVILED CRABMEAT
155

KITTY'S SWORDFISH WITH
MUSTARD CREAM SAUCE
159

OYSTER PIE ON
THE HALF-SHELL
162

CRAB CAKES
166

BUNKY'S "BALLED SHRUMP"
(AKA BOILED SHRIMP)
169

BUNKY COOKS SOME
SOFT-SHELL CRABS
172

TARTAR SAUCE
173

SEAFOOD

The reason the Lowcountry is called "low" is because it's so close to sea level. Charleston is not just on the ocean, it's practically in the ocean. The Atlantic is everywhere you look, including your yard on a king tide. South Carolina has more tidal inlets than any state other than Florida, and growing up, I never had to walk very far with my rod. My happiest memories were fishing with Dad in our little 17-foot tri-hull Renken bowrider. On Saturday mornings, we would "crank it up and head for Spain," though we mostly ended up in the Stono River. We had a book called *The Saltwater Fisherman's Bible*, and I read the covers off it.

There is nothing like the electric feeling of a strike on your line. "The tug is the drug." I am hooked for life. And for me, there is no meal more satisfying than the one I caught that day. If you can't get a fish on the hook, there is always shrimp in the net or crabs in the pot or oysters on the bank. The waters of Charleston are teeming with seafood, and there are thousands of ways to fix it. Here are just a few of our favorites.

Tight lines! • **STEPHEN**

SEA BASS
in White Wine Butter

STEPHEN • *When I was nine, my father, my brother Bill, and I took our small boat down the Stono River to the Kiawah to fish. It was late fall— quiet and the water was glass with a dusting of mist. We hit on a school of bass. I remember that across the creek, a romp of otters (yes, "romp" is the term) was catching their own dinner. Competition. I thought the otters looked cute. Bill said they're aggressive and they bite and that if they got in our boat, I should get in the water. I've never fact-checked him on that.*

When Mom saw the fish, she pulled down Charleston Receipts, *and here we are today.*

EVIE • *This is an old Charleston receipt. My mother often made this for a summer supper party, and even if I was too young to be a guest at the table, I would be allowed to have a bite in the kitchen and I loved it. I know cheese on fish may sound odd, but it adds an unexpected richness that makes this fish dish really unique.*

> *tip*—As you lower the fillets into the dish, place the end of the fillet nearest you into the butter first as you lower it so that any butter that splashes will head away from you—not onto you.

Makes 4 servings

Salt and freshly ground pepper

4 sea bass fillets, or any flaky white fish (about 10 ounces each)

8 tablespoons (1 stick) unsalted butter

½ cup dry white wine

Juice of 1 lemon

Enough grated Parmesan cheese to cover the fillets generously (about ¾ cup)

Heat the broiler with an oven rack in the middle position. Salt and pepper the bass fillets on both sides.

Put the butter in a baking dish large enough to hold all 4 fillets. (Make sure the dish is OK to put under the broiler—i.e., flameproof.) Set the dish under the broiler to melt the butter. When the butter is bubbling but not browned, carefully slip in the fillets and return the dish to the broiler. Baste the fillets with the butter in the dish after a minute. Then broil until the fillets are about halfway cooked, about 5 minutes. Keep the stove vent on high for this one!

Sprinkle the wine and lemon juice over the fillets, then sprinkle enough grated Parm over them to coat generously. Return to the broiler until the cheese is melted and golden brown, about 2 minutes.

Remove from the oven and move the fillets to plates. Spoon some of the butter in the dish over each serving.

We love to serve this with Red Rice (page 182). If there is any butter left over, save it to sauté shrimp, or to serve with rice, or . . .

Panfried
SPOT TAIL BASS

STEPHEN • *This fish has firm flesh that stands up to flipping in the pan. It has a lot of names—spot tail, channel bass, red drum, red fish—and is larger than my other favorite inshore catch, sea trout. Sea bass are also a good fight on the line. As our friend Amy Sedaris would say, "Exciting to catch. Delicious to eat!" Because they are relatively large, they are easy to clean. One large spot tail will feed two, a few will feed a group. Serve this with Red Rice (page 182), and you will be excused to go fishing any time you like.*

EVIE • *Along with impressing me with his shrimp-paste-making abilities, Stephen won me over early on by cleaning the fish that we would catch (even the fish that I caught—what a gentleman). And he would fry them up as well! Like the spot tail bass, I was hooked!*

tips—This makes a heap of seasoned coating. After mixing it, spoon about ½ cup of the mix into a shallow bowl and set the rest aside. Dredge the fillets, adding a little more of the mix if needed. Stored in a cool, dark place, the leftover coating will keep for months.

•

As you lower the fillets into the pan, place the end of the fillet nearest you into the oil first as you lower it so that any oil that splashes will head away from you—not onto you.

Makes 2 to 4 servings

2½ cups fine yellow cornmeal

½ cup all-purpose flour

1 tablespoon salt

1 tablespoon freshly ground pepper

1 tablespoon paprika

1 teaspoon garlic powder

Neutral oil, such as vegetable or canola oil, for shallow-frying

2 to 4 spot tail bass fillets (about 8 ounces each), skinned (or other firm fish fillets, such as halibut or pollock)

Lemon wedges for serving

Tartar Sauce, homemade (page 173) or store-bought

Stir together the cornmeal, flour, salt, pepper, paprika, and garlic powder, in a medium bowl.

Pour ½ inch of oil into a large, heavy skillet. Heat over medium heat to 375°F. If you don't have a deep-frying thermometer, a sprinkling of the cornmeal coating should sizzle and brown right away when the oil is ready.

While the oil is heating, dredge the fillets in the cornmeal mixture to coat them well. Line a baking sheet with paper towels. Gently slip the fillets in the hot oil.

Keep a close eye on the fish, as it will cook quickly. When the bottom is golden brown, slide a spatula under the fillets one at a time and roll them over. (Flipping the fillets may break them, but they'll still be tasty.) When the second side is golden, remove the fillets and drain them on the paper towels for just a moment before serving with lemon wedges and tartar sauce.

FLOUNDER STUFFED
with Deviled Crabmeat

EVIE • *If you are having a dinner party and are feeling ambitious, try this. I know it sounds intimidating, but it is surprisingly simple to make. Plus, it looks very impressive. If you have access to a good seafood store, ask if they will sell you a whole fresh flounder, deboned and head removed, but still in one piece (see Notes). If not, then simply buy four flounder fillets and roll those around some of the filling (see Notes). And remember, the deviled crabmeat is also delicious served on its own.*

STEPHEN • *When I was at Northwestern University, I had a class called "Archetypal and Psychological Approaches to Literature." The professor was a Jungian analyst named Leland Roloff. Thank goodness he didn't run a cult, because I would have shaved my head and moved to the compound. One of the works we "approached" was* Grimms' Fairy Tales. *On the day he taught "The Fisherman and His Wife," he brought another Jungian along to explicate the archetypes (reading this intro counts as SAT training). The fish in this fairy tale, a fish that grants wishes, is a flounder. When Professor Roloff asked us to consider the strange nature of a flounder, spending its whole life on the bottom of the ocean floor, with both eyes staring up from one side of its flat body, I raised my hand to tell him that flounder actually don't start their life flat. A newborn flounder lives throughout the water column and moves toward the bottom as one eye migrates to the other side of the fish and it flattens out. After a long pause he said, "How do you know this?" I said, "I grew up fishing for flounder." The Jungians stared at each other for a moment, then the guest lecturer said, "This changes everything." I don't know what it changed, but this recipe is good.*

(Spoiler: The fisherman wished for too much and lost everything.)

continued →

THE CRABMEAT FILLING

3 tablespoons unsalted butter

2 tablespoons all-purpose flour

½ cup whole milk, warmed

1 teaspoon Dijon mustard

1 teaspoon salt

1 teaspoon lemon juice, or more to taste

½ teaspoon Worcestershire sauce

¼ teaspoon garlic salt

Pinch of freshly ground pepper

Dash of Tabasco or other hot sauce

½ pound crabmeat (claw meat is fine), picked over for bits of shell

½ cup panko

THE FLOUNDER

2 tablespoons (¼ stick) unsalted butter, melted, plus more, unmelted, for the baking sheet

1 lemon

One whole 2- to 2½-pound flounder, prepared for stuffing (see Notes)

Salt and freshly ground pepper

Lemon wedges for serving

Make the filling: Heat the butter in a small saucepan over medium heat. When it is foaming, whisk in the flour. Reduce the heat a little and cook the roux, whisking often, for 2 minutes. Drizzle in the warm milk, whisking constantly, and bring to a boil, then reduce the heat to a simmer and cook for 2 minutes. Scrape into a large bowl.

Whisk the mustard, salt, lemon juice, Worcestershire sauce, garlic salt, pepper, and hot sauce into the milk mixture. Gently fold in the crabmeat and panko. Set aside.

Heat the oven to 350°F with a rack in the center position.

Make the flounder: Line a baking sheet with aluminum foil and butter the foil (see Notes). Halve the lemon, thinly slice one half, and set the other half aside.

Season the inside of the cleaned flounder generously with salt and pepper and the juice from the reserved half lemon. Move the flounder to the prepared baking sheet. Lift back the two top fillets (i.e., "open up the book"). Cover the bottom fillets with two-thirds of the crabmeat filling, mounding it slightly. Fold the top fillets over the filling, letting a little of the filling peep through. Make a line of the remaining filling down the center of the flounder (over the filling that's peeping through). Brush the top of the flounder and the filling generously with the 2 tablespoons melted butter. Overlap half of the lemon slices on either side of the filling. Tent the baking sheet with another sheet of aluminum foil.

Bake the flounder for 15 minutes. Remove the foil, baste the fish with some of the butter from the pan, and return to the oven, uncovered. Bake until the fish is cooked through and the filling is very warm, about 15 minutes. Let stand for 5 minutes before serving.

• A flounder boned and left whole will certainly be a special order. But if you can find a good fishmonger, ask them to clean and dress a 2- to 2½-pound flounder and then debone it while leaving the flounder intact and ready for stuffing. If you can't find a good seafood shop to do that, here's how to handle the preparation of a cleaned flounder, with the head removed, for stuffing: Working with the darker side of the fish facing up and using a fillet knife, cut carefully down to the bone along the "seam" between the two top fillets. Still using the fillet knife, cut away the top fillets from the bone, working from the center toward the edges of the fish. (You'll be opening the fillets like a book.) Be sure to free the fillets all the way to the edges of the fish but leaving them still attached. Work the fillet knife under the bones to completely free the bottom fillets and separate them from all the bones. Trim any excess bones from the top and bottom fillets as needed.

• Choose a baking sheet with a rim (as opposed to a cookie sheet) that is large enough to hold the flounder very comfortably. Remember, you will be moving the very delicate whole cooked fish, so leave yourself some room to maneuver.

variation
STUFFED FLOUNDER FILLETS

Substitute four large, about 5-ounce, flounder fillets for the whole fish. Prepare the filling as above. Lay out the fillets on the prepared baking sheet. Season the fillets generously with salt and pepper, squeeze the lemon half over them, and brush with some of the melted butter. Top the fillets with the crabmeat filling, dividing it evenly and keeping the filling more toward the thicker end of the fillets. Fold the thinner end of the fillets over the filling and secure them in place with toothpicks. Season the top of the fillets with salt and pepper, brush with the remaining butter, and sprinkle a generous amount of paprika over them. Cover the baking sheet loosely with foil and bake until the fillets are fully cooked and the filling is heated through, about 20 minutes. Let stand for 5 minutes before serving.

KITTY'S SWORDFISH
with Mustard Cream Sauce

EVIE • *In the summers when our children were little, we would drive from New Jersey to Charleston. It was an odyssey: two adults, three small children, one dog, lots of suitcases and beach toys, and at least three bikes strapped to the back of the car. Frankly, there weren't enough Harry Potter books on tape to keep us going all fourteen hours, so . . . we would break up the trip in DC, where we have a lot of family. We would often stay with Stephen's brother and sister-in-law, Ed and Kitty. We would limp out of the car with battle scars from sibling fights, or car sickness, or traffic, or whatever else had gone down on the trip, and a glass of cold wine and a hot meal would be waiting for us. Kitty often served us this delicious swordfish, and it quickly restored our faith that we would, in fact, survive the drive and all would be well once more. I challenge you to find a hotel anywhere with better food—or nicer linens, for that matter—than those at Ed and Kitty's.*

STEPHEN • *Truth be told, halfway between New York and Charleston is over three hours south of Ed and Kitty's. We just couldn't pass up this swordfish . . . or those linens!*

> *tip*—All broilers are different. If you see your butter starting to brown too much in the first few minutes, lower the rack (carefully!) one notch.

Makes 4 servings

4 medium swordfish steaks (about 1 inch thick and 12 ounces each)

Salt and freshly ground pepper

12 tablespoons (1½ sticks) unsalted butter, cut into little pieces

⅓ cup dry white wine

⅓ cup heavy cream

1½ tablespoons Dijon mustard

1 rounded teaspoon drained and coarsely chopped nonpareil capers (optional)

Preheat the oven to broil, or the highest possible temperature available, with rack one level down from the top. Line up the swordfish steaks on a baking sheet and season them generously on both sides with salt and pepper. Dot each with 2½ tablespoons of the butter.

Broil the fish for approximately 5 minutes on each side, basting with the butter in the pan before you flip them. When it's time to flip, the butter should be a rich, nutty brown.

While the fish finishes broiling, stir together the wine, cream, mustard, and capers, if using, in a small saucepan and bring to a boil over medium-high heat, then lower the heat and gently simmer until the sauce is reduced by half, about 5 minutes. Season with salt and pepper to taste (you may not need any salt because of the mustard and capers). Remove from the heat and whisk in the remaining 2 tablespoons butter.

Serve topped with mustard cream sauce.

OYSTER PIE
on the Half-Shell

EVIE · *We are fortunate to have lots of family around the table for most of our holiday meals. Often my sister, Madeleine, will make an authentic Charleston dish called oyster pie. My family always had it at Thanksgiving when I was growing up, and Madeleine has continued the family tradition. Cooking the pie often takes much longer than we think, however, and it sometimes makes much more than we need. So we have transferred the recipe to the half-shell. The cracker-crumb-and-butter crust is still there, just now on each individual oyster, which increases the crumb-to-oyster ratio in a good way.*

STEPHEN · *When we make oyster pie, we always have lots of leftovers—not because it isn't good, but because making it always takes so much longer than you planned that it's never ready on time, and you've had second helpings of every other dish by the time the pie gets out of the oven. This recipe fixes that timing issue. Also, individual baked oysters make a great addition to cocktail hour, which is where dinner ends for us many nights.*

Makes 4 servings

4 tablespoons (½ stick) unsalted butter

Juice of ½ lemon

1 teaspoon Worcestershire sauce

1 cup Ritz (or similar) cracker crumbs (about 25 crackers)

¼ cup chopped green onions (about 1 large green onion)

3 tablespoons chopped fresh flat-leaf parsley

½ teaspoon dry mustard

16 oysters, shucked (save the deeper bottom shells!)

Heat the oven to 450°F with a rack in the top position. Lightly crumple a long sheet of aluminum foil. Uncrumple the foil and use it to line a small baking sheet. The little crumples will help keep the oysters upright as they cook.

Melt the butter in a small saucepan over low heat. Remove from the heat, stir in the lemon juice and Worcestershire sauce, and set aside for a minute.

Stir the cracker crumbs, green onions, parsley, and dry mustard together in a large bowl. Pour the seasoned melted butter into the crumb mixture and stir until the crumbs are evenly buttered.

Make sure the oysters are nestled comfortably in their half-shells. Top the oysters with the crumbs, dividing them evenly and tamping the topping down very lightly. Set the filled shells on the foil, wiggling them a little into the crumples to keep them steady.

Bake until the oysters are cooked and the tops are browned, about 12 minutes. Let stand for about 3 minutes before serving.

OYSTERS ON THE HALF-SHELL PROTOCOL

If shucking your own oysters, leave the oysters in the deeper bottom shells, and remember to cut the oysters free from the shells before baking. If you have your seafood supplier shuck them for you, ask them to save as much of the oyster liquor as possible, as well as the bottom shells for baking. Spoon a little of the liquor over the oysters in the shell before topping with the crumb mix.

CRAB CAKES

EVIE • *We love crab cakes. But often a receipt will call for too much "stuff" and not enough crab. This one has the correct balance. Just enough "stuff" to bind the crabmeat and allow it to fry up into tasty cakes. We cook them at night for dinner and then sometimes, if there are any left over, eat them for breakfast. Yummy both ways*

STEPHEN • *Like shrimp, crabs are all over the Lowcountry. I don't know a creek that doesn't have a crab pot in it. The pots are marked by buoys—sometimes a brightly colored float, sometimes an empty resealed Clorox bottle. You want to drive around the buoys. That's a hard lesson to learn when the rope gets twisted around your prop. If you just want a few crabs for dinner, tie a chicken neck to a string, drop it off the side of a boat or dock, and after (let's say) five minutes, slooooowly draw it back up. As it gets to the surface, you'll see the crab nibbling away with a firm grip, and he won't know the jig is up until your net slides under him.*

About this crab-cake-for-breakfast situation—nothing better. Especially if the night before was thirsty work. Put the leftover crab cake in a pan, and as it fries, break it up like a hash, then pop a fried egg on that bad boy, and you're starting the day right!

> *tip*—An old-school cast-iron griddle is a perfect way to cook these. All 6 cakes will most likely fit at once and, because a griddle doesn't have sides, the cakes will be easier to turn. Wait for the griddle to heat before adding the butter and oil. Jockey the cakes around once or twice as they cook so they brown evenly.

Makes 6 large crab cakes

2 large eggs

1 tablespoon mayonnaise

1 teaspoon sherry (optional)

1 teaspoon Worcestershire sauce (optional)

1 teaspoon salt

⅛ teaspoon freshly ground pepper

Dash of cayenne pepper

⅔ cup panko

1 small onion, minced (about ⅓ cup)

2 tablespoons chopped fresh flat-leaf parsley

1 pound fresh crabmeat, picked over for bits of shell

2 tablespoons unsalted butter

2 tablespoons vegetable oil

Beat the eggs, mayonnaise, sherry and Worcestershire sauce, if using, salt, black pepper, and cayenne together in a medium bowl until well blended. Stir in the panko, onion, and parsley. Lastly, gently fold in the crabmeat. Refrigerate for about 15 minutes to firm up the mix.

Using ½ cup of the mix for each, form 6 cakes about ½ inch thick. You will probably need to fry these in batches (see Tip): Heat half the butter and oil in a large skillet over medium-low heat until the butter stops foaming. Slip 3 of the cakes into the hot fat and cook until the bottoms are golden brown, about 5 minutes. Flip and brown the other side. If you like, keep those cakes warm on a baking sheet in an oven heated to 200°F while you fry the last 3 cakes. Serve hot.

Bunky's "Balled Shrump" (AKA BOILED SHRIMP)

BUNKY · *Shrimp (or "shrump" in the local dialect) is king and the base for so much of the Lowcountry's seafood culture and history. Local shrimp are prized for their freshness, size, and great flavor.*

Like most foods, the fresher you can get the product, the better it will taste, and the better it will be for you. If you can, go to the docks and buy either right from the boat or at the closest fish market to the docks. Always check to see if the shrimp are fresh, with no dark spots starting to show on the shell. They should smell briny, not fishy or of ammonia.

For a lesser dollar amount per pound, you can buy them with the heads still on. This is quite foreign to many, as one almost never sees a shrimp with its head on in a restaurant or even a seafood store here. Buying them right off the boat or dock is usually the only way to get them with the heads on, but that adds great flavor to the shrimp when they are boiled or steamed. The heads and shells can also be used to create a fantastic stock.

Shrimp are graded depending on size—specifically, on how many it takes to make up a pound. For example, if you have 31–35 count shrimp, then 31–35 of these crustaceans will weigh a pound. The higher the count, the smaller the shrimp. Thirty-one count are considered large shrimp, while 21–25 count are considered jumbo. (Always go by the number count; terms like "jumbo" and "colossal," for example, can be misleading.)

The most basic way of cooking shrimp, and the way most are served, is boiled (or steamed) shrimp. Here is a quick and simple recipe.

Makes 4 to 6 large servings

Large (8- to 12-quart) stockpot filled about halfway with water

¼ cup salt

Freshly ground pepper

2 lemons, cut into halves

2 tablespoons coriander seeds

2 tablespoons red pepper flakes

2 bay leaves

4 pounds fresh 31–35 count shrimp in the shell

Bring the water to a boil and add all the ingredients except the shrimp. Let the flavors steep in the water for a few minutes while you bring it back to a boil. Slip the shrimp into the boiling water. For the 31-count shrimp, we will cook for 3½ minutes. For smaller shrimp, the amount of time needs to be dropped back to 3 minutes. If you have 24-count or larger, you may go as long as 4 minutes, but no longer. DO NOT OVERCOOK YOUR SHRIMP—you will not be happy. They must be strained and cooled down as quickly as possible after cooking. I like to toss them a bit in the colander to help cool them down and keep them from cooking further. If you want to top the shrimp with spices, salt, or something like Old Bay, this is a good time to do that.

Serve with lemon wedges, melted butter, or a cocktail sauce. Peel, eat, and enjoy.

Bunky Cooks Some
SOFT-SHELL CRABS

BUNKY • *Soft-shell crabs are a delicacy available fresh only twice a year, when the water temperature hits about 70°F. This happens usually in April and October here in the Lowcountry of South Carolina.*

Soft-shells can be sautéed, deep-fried, or even grilled. For this recipe, I sauté them in butter and a little oil in a large cast-iron skillet. If you don't have a cast-iron skillet, use the heaviest 10- to 12-inch pan you can find.

When buying your softies, make sure they are alive. If they are not moving, then choose ones that are. Your fishmonger will usually have already slit the ends of the carapace (shell) so that access to the gills— also known as "dead men" or "dead man's fingers"—is easier. Remove the gills by snipping the wider ends with scissors and pulling them out. Also remove the face of the crab by cutting straight across, just behind the eyes. It's best to do all of this only when you are ready to cook the crabs.

Makes 2 generous servings or 4 sandwiches

2 tablespoons unsalted butter

2 tablespoons vegetable or canola oil

4 fresh live soft-shell crabs, cleaned (see above)

Salt and freshly ground pepper

Old Bay or similar seasoning (optional)

½ cup all-purpose flour

Tartar Sauce (recipe follows), your favorite hot sauce, or lemon wedges

Heat the butter and oil in a large cast-iron skillet over low heat. While your skillet is warming up, dry the prepared crabs with a paper towel. Season the crabs with salt and pepper to taste, along with some Old Bay seasoning, if using. Dredge the crabs in the flour, then shake or tap them to get rid of excess flour.

Increase the heat under the pan to medium, and when the butter is foaming, add the crabs. Fry them, turning once, until nice and golden brown on both sides and cooked through.

Unlike "regular" crabs, the entire soft-shell crab can be eaten—legs, claws, shell, etc. Enjoy with tartar sauce, hot sauce, or lemon wedges.

NOTE

• Blue claw crabs are found in brackish waters in the Atlantic Ocean from Nova Scotia to well along the South American coast. Soft-shell crabs are blue claws that are molting—that is, shedding their very hard shells to reveal a much softer, almost paper-thin shell. Before those soft shells start to harden, the crabs—shells, claws, and all other bits—can be eaten in their entirety. Soft-shell season depends on where you are—the Lowcountry might see the first soft shells of the year in late April, Chesapeake Bay more like May. Not on the East Coast? Locals Seafood in North Carolina offers nationwide shipping.

TARTAR SAUCE

Makes about ⅔ cup

3 tablespoons finely diced
dill pickles

2 tablespoons chopped fresh
flat-leaf parsley

1 tablespoon drained capers

½ cup mayo

A couple dashes of hot sauce,
if you're feeling it

FANCY

Grated zest of 1 lemon

FANCIER

2 teaspoons chopped fresh
tarragon

Substitute cornichons for
the pickle

Make a little pile of the pickles,
parsley, and capers on a cutting
board. Chop them all together
to get the flavors good and
mixed. Stir the chopped-up
little pile into the mayo and
dash in the hot sauce, if using.
For the fancy/fancier versions,
stir those ingredients in.
Tartar sauce will keep in the
refrigerator for up to 2 weeks.

RED RICE
182

HOPPIN' JOHN
198

BALSAMIC
PEARL ONIONS
183

SCALLOPED
POTATOES
199

ARUGULA
PINE NUT SALAD
186

JIM'S SPAGHETTI
SQUASH CASSEROLE
202

WHIPPED SWEET
POTATOES WITH
BROWN SUGAR
CRUMBLE
188

CRISPY HOT-HONEY
BRUSSELS SPROUTS
203

CLAUS'S
COLLARD GREENS
204

MARY'S POTATO SALAD
189

HEIRLOOM TOMATO
SALAD WITH
PISTOU PROVENÇAL
AND BURRATA
191

WILD RICE WITH
CRANBERRIES AND
TOASTED ALMONDS
206

BUTTERMILK
CORNBREAD
208

GLAZED PARSNIPS
192

SMASHED POTATOES
195

LULU'S JOHNS ISLAND
TOMATO SHED PIE
210

CAULIFLOWER PUREE
196

SOURDOUGH BREAD
212

VEGETABLES, SIDES, AND ONE OTHER THING

It took us a long time to figure out what to call this eclectic chapter. I was pushing for "lots of yummy stuff," because this might be my favorite chapter in the book. Give me a bowl of rice or a plate of Brussels sprouts, and I am a happy camper—though that wasn't always the case. When I was a young girl, my family had our large meal in the middle of the day. My father, who was a lawyer, would walk home from his office on Broad Street at around 2:00 p.m. He would join my mother, my sister, and me for a proper meal in the dining room. We usually had some sort of meat, often roast beef and gravy, as well as rice. (Charlestonians eat a lot of rice.) But we also ate okra or peas or fresh tomatoes. And I didn't like any of them! My father still laughs at the memory of me as

a six-year-old saying very sweetly, "Daddy, would you like some of my peas?" He never fell for it, and I had to sneak them to the dog. I still don't like peas or okra, to be honest, but bring on just about any other vegetable.

For this chapter, we have chosen our favorite accompaniments to go along with an entrée of meat or seafood, but they are also delicious served all on their own. You might notice that a lot of these receipts are rather starchy—that was not intentional, but I suspect it does present an accurate portrait of our diet. Don't get me wrong, we love roasted broccoli or a good veggie stir-fry, but when we think of our favorite go-tos, the foods that make us happy and that we like to share with our friends, these are the ones. • **EVIE**

RED RICE

STEPHEN • *My love of red rice started at Stiles Point Elementary School on James Island, South Carolina. The cafeteria served it just about every day, and that was fine with me. I've had a lot since then, but this comes closest to the deep savory sweetness that those lunch ladies somehow whipped up in barrel-sized batches. I came up with this version after food writer Alison Roman and I made her caramelized shallot pasta sauce on* The Late Show. *There was something about the aroma, both jammy and tangy, that told me it would make a killer rice. I love being right.*

*
pictured on
pages 184–85

EVIE • *Red rice is a classic Southern receipt, and another example of the enormous influence of West African culture on Lowcountry cuisine. I have been making the version from the* Charleston Receipts Cookbook *for decades. But that calls for bacon and bacon grease, and I don't mess with that anymore. Thankfully, Stephen substituted smoked salt and anchovies, and ta-da! Even better than the original!*

Makes about 6 cups; 8 servings

¼ cup olive oil

6 medium shallots, finely chopped (about 1 cup)

2 teaspoons smoked salt, such as Bulls Bay (see Notes), or as needed

1 teaspoon freshly ground pepper

One 2-ounce tin anchovies, drained

One 4.5-ounce tube double-concentrated tomato paste or ½ cup regular tomato paste

1 teaspoon red pepper flakes

2 cups Charleston Gold aromatic rice or other long-grain rice

3 cups water (see Notes)

A few tablespoons chopped fresh flat-leaf parsley

Heat the olive oil in a heavy 3- to 4-quart saucepan or a Dutch oven over medium-low heat. Add the shallots and cook, stirring occasionally, until golden, about 8 minutes. Season with the smoked salt and pepper. Stir the anchovies into the shallots and keep stirring until they melt away. Add the tomato paste and red pepper flakes and cook until the paste turns a nice jammy red, about 4 minutes.

Stir in the rice and water and season with more salt. (Dip a finger in to make sure it's seasoned to your liking.) Heat the water to a boil, give the rice a big stir, and reduce the heat to a very low simmer. Cover the pan and cook, undisturbed, for 12 minutes.

Cut off the heat and leave the cover on for an additional 8 minutes. Then (and only then!) lift the lid and fluff with a fork. Sprinkle the parsley over the top and serve—hopefully with the Sea Bass in White Wine Butter on page 150.

NOTES

• Bulls Bay smoked salt starts out as sea salt harvested from the waters of Bulls Bay on the South Carolina coast. Oak-smoking gives the salt its particular hearty flavor. Bulls Bay salt can be found online.

• Different types of rice may need different amounts of water. Use the cooking instructions on the package of rice as a guide. Because the tomato/shallot jam is semi-liquid, you may find that you want to reduce the amount of water.

Balsamic PEARL ONIONS

STEPHEN • *Pearl onions are a staple of holiday dinners, but these are fantastic any time. I first turned to this recipe because I love peas and pearl onions, but Evie considers peas in any form a torture for the damned. I had already bought the pearl onions, so here's the result.*

EVIE • *Don't even talk to me about peas! YUCK! But these pearl onions are really delicious (just keep those peas out of there!).*

✳ pictured on pages 184–85

Makes 6 servings

4 cups pearl onions (about 1½ 14-ounce bags of frozen; you can peel fresh ones if you want, but I can't imagine why)

1 cup balsamic vinegar

¼ cup extra-virgin olive oil

1 tablespoon honey

2 cloves garlic, finely minced or crushed

Salt and freshly ground pepper

Heat the oven to 400°F with a rack in the lowest position. Toss the onions, balsamic, olive oil, and honey together in an 11 × 7-inch (or similar size) baking dish. Bake for 30 minutes, stirring occasionally.

Stir in the garlic and bake until the onions are well browned, tender, and coated with a rich glaze, 15 to 30 minutes. The onions should be soft and sweet—like peas, but not at all. Salt and pepper to taste.

ARUGULA PINE NUT SALAD

STEPHEN • *As a young actor in Chicago, I waited tables for many years at many restaurants. My longest waiting gig, and by far the best, was at an Italian trattoria in the River North area called Scoozi. It was a barn of a place, rimmed with booths and banquettes, with a high vaulted ceiling, open rafters, hard tile floors, and loyal customers addicted to the zucchini haystacks and the cracker-thin pizzas. High-quality Italian food, something beyond pizza and spaghetti, was enjoying a moment in the spotlight, and I learned a lot. For instance, this was back in the '80s, when arugula was exotic for Americans (or at least for Midwesterners), pine nuts sounded like a brand of trail mix, and Parmesan was something you shook out of a can from the Good People© at Kraft™. This is the salad that taught me otherwise.*

Pine nuts, sometimes labeled "pignoli," have a sweet crunch when lightly toasted in a dry pan. The amounts, like all the amounts in this barely-a-recipe, are malleable to the point of meaninglessness. I say ¼ cup of pine nuts is enough for 2 servings. Where do I find the courage? Place them in a dry pan over medium heat, and don't go anywhere! They seem to do nothing for the first few minutes, but shake the pan occasionally, as the browning happens on the underside and when it goes, it goes fast. You want a light brown/tan. As soon as you achieve the desired toasting, take them off the burner and out of the pan, or they will burn in the residual heat. Place the arugula in a bowl. A wooden bowl is nice. About one fistful per serving works, I think. Baby arugula has the best mix of peppery and sweet, if you can find it. Toss it with a nice garlicky vinaigrette, then sprinkle on the Parmesan after. The vinaigrette will help the cheese cling, rather than settle on the bottom of the salad bowl. Toss on the cooled pine nuts and ecco la! *My last-meal salad.*

EVIE • *When Stephen and I first started dating, I was living in New York, and he was in Chicago. We dated long-distance for over a year, but after a while, we thought we should try living in the same city to see how that went. I offered to move to Chicago. I was intrigued to try out the Midwest. But one thing worried me—where would I find arugula? I was accustomed to stopping by a bodega on my way home from the subway and picking up a fresh bundle, along with the* New York Times *and some fig bars. Did Chicago even have those things? Stephen promised to make me this salad as a solution. It worked. I moved, we got married, and the salad has been with us ever since.*

WHIPPED SWEET POTATOES
with Brown Sugar Crumble

EVIE • *The wonderful thing about this receipt is that you could easily serve it for dessert. The sweet potatoes are so light and the topping adds just the right amount of sugary crust; it's like a pie without the pastry shell. We have this dish on our table every Christmas and Thanksgiving, and we always run out. It is a family favorite for sure.*

STEPHEN • *The debate when the kids were younger was: a melted marshmallow top or brown-sugar pecan crust. I'm glad the crust won out, because with the marshmallow, it was very hard to pretend you weren't just freebasing pie filling.*

Makes 8 servings

THE POTATOES

3 large sweet potatoes, washed

8 tablespoons (1 stick) butter, at room temperature, plus a little more for the pan

¼ cup whole milk

1 teaspoon vanilla extract, or more to taste

Salt

THE TOPPING

1 cup packed brown sugar

1 cup chopped pecans

⅓ cup melted butter (about 5 tablespoons)

⅓ cup all-purpose flour

NOTE

• This is the perfect make-ahead dish. Prepare the filling and scrape it into the buttered dish; refrigerate. Make the topping and refrigerate separately. Pull both from the refrigerator, combine, and bake as directed.

Heat the oven to 400°F with a rack in the center position. Put the sweet potatoes on a small baking sheet lined with aluminum foil or parchment paper. Bake until the sweet potatoes are very tender, about 1½ hours. Remove from the oven and let them stand until cool enough to handle but still pretty warm.

Meanwhile, reduce the oven temp to 350°F. Lightly butter a deep 8 × 10-inch (or similar size) casserole dish and set aside.

Pull the skins off the sweet potatoes and put the potatoes in a large bowl. You should have approximately 4 cups. Add the butter, milk, and vanilla and, using a handheld mixer, beat until fairly smooth. (You can use a stand mixer for this instead.) Season with salt. Scrape the sweet potatoes into the prepared baking dish, smooth out the top, and bake for 15 to 20 minutes, just until the edges start to set up.

Meanwhile, make the topping: In a medium bowl, rub together the brown sugar, pecans, melted butter, and flour until the butter is thoroughly incorporated and the topping is crumbly.

Remove the baking dish from the oven and crumble the topping over the sweet potatoes. Bake for 15 to 20 minutes longer, or until barely set and golden brown on edges. Let sit for 5 to 10 minutes before serving.

Mary's
POTATO SALAD

STEPHEN • *This is one of the recipes that was a simple yet sturdy mainstay of my mother's repertoire.*

I would never have remembered the vinaigrette if my sister Mary hadn't recently brought it to our July 4th party, but the acid and herbs make an often-leaden side dish bright. It was all gone before the fireworks.

EVIE • *Although we have titled this Mary's potato salad, I think of it as Colbert potato salad. It beat out McGee potato salad for inclusion in the book, much to my father's chagrin. To be fair, my father can't quite remember the receipt for McGee potato salad except to say it is equal parts potatoes, mayonnaise, and vinegar. Yikes! This one is much better!*

STEPHEN • *Just texted with Mary. She says Mom didn't use dill. I'm leaving it in. We can fight it out next 4th of July.*

Makes about 6 cups; 10 servings

Salt

1½ pounds new potatoes, cut into quarters

⅓ cup light vinaigrette

½ cup mayonnaise

1 cup diced celery (about 1 large stalk)

¼ cup finely chopped fresh dill

Bring 2½ quarts of salted water to boil in a large pot. Add the potatoes and boil until tender, about 10 minutes (test with a fork).

Drain the potatoes. Give the vinaigrette a good whisking in a large bowl, then add the cooked potatoes and toss gently. Set aside. If there is a little pooling of the vinaigrette, don't worry—as the potatoes cool, they will drink it up. Toss again after a few minutes. Let stand until cool.

Add the mayonnaise, celery, and dill to the potatoes, tossing until all the ingredients are thoroughly mixed. Refrigerate, uncovered, until chilled, then mix again before serving. The potato salad will keep in the refrigerator for up to several days.

HEIRLOOM TOMATO SALAD
with Pistou Provençal and Burrata

EVIE • *Here is another of our favorite dishes that Jane Satow introduced to us in France. The mix of yellow, red, and green from the heirloom tomatoes makes this unique and more appetizing than a simple tomato salad. The Provençal pistou is light and basil-y without the richness of cheese, but you can always substitute regular pesto if you prefer.*

Makes 4 to 8 servings, depending on the number of tomatoes (there will be enough pistou for 8 servings)

THE PISTOU
2 cups lightly packed fresh basil leaves (no stems)

½ cup extra-virgin olive oil

6 cloves garlic

1 teaspoon sea salt, preferably fleur de sel

THE SALAD
2 medium heirloom tomatoes per person, cored and cut into relatively equal-sized wedges

1 (or 2) burrata

Toasted pine nuts (see Arugula Pine Nut Salad, page 186, for toasting instructions)

Fresh basil sprigs, for garnish

A large platter that gives the variety of tomatoes a chance to shine (and makes the salad easier to serve) is a nice touch.

Make the pistou: Put the basil leaves, olive oil, garlic, and salt in a food processor and pulse until you have a creamy paste about the consistency of a milk shake.

Assemble the salad: Arrange the tomatoes around the edges of a platter, leaving a space in the middle for the burrata. Drizzle the pistou over the tomato wedges. Add a ripe burrata cheese (or two, depending on your crowd) to the center. Scatter the toasted pine nuts over everything and garnish with basil sprigs.

tip—Summer vine-ripened heirloom tomatoes of different colors are what makes this salad so beautiful and delicious.

Glazed
PARSNIPS

STEPHEN • *This was a farmers' market special. I bought a bunch of lovely parsnips on a whim, but I had never cooked (or I think eaten) them. So, I stared at them on the kitchen counter for a while. I thought that caramelizing them would be nice, since I didn't like the color. Parsnips look like carrots for the color-blind. I turned on the oven and let miso and maple do the rest.*

EVIE • *I am not even sure I had eaten parsnips before Stephen made me this dish. I can't believe what I was missing. Think of all the parsnips I could have been eating when instead I had sweet potatoes or carrots. The miso and syrup really make this a showstopper of sweetness with a tang of umami: delicious!*

Makes 4 servings

1 pound not-too-large parsnips, peeled and topped

3 tablespoons extra-virgin olive oil

1 tablespoon maple syrup

1 tablespoon white miso paste

2 cloves garlic, finely chopped

1 tablespoon water

Salt and freshly ground pepper

Heat the oven to 400°F with a rack in the center position. Line a baking sheet with aluminum foil or parchment paper.

Quarter the peeled parsnips lengthwise. Toss them with the olive oil and spread them out on the baking sheet—not too close, or they will steam instead of brown. Bake until almost but not quite tender in the thickest part, about 20 minutes.

While the parsnips are cooking, stir the maple syrup, miso paste, garlic, and water together in a small bowl until smooth.

Brush the maple/miso mixture liberally onto the (mostly) cooked parsnips. Continue baking until the parsnips are fork-tender and the glaze is lightly browned, about 5 minutes. Sprinkle the parsnips with salt and pepper—light on the salt though, the miso has enough salt of its own. Adding candied peppers is optional but adds a nice touch of color. Enjoy!

Smashed
POTATOES

STEPHEN • *My mom taught me to love new potatoes, boiled to tender, lightly mashed, skins on, buttered, and salted. I was never sure what the "new" referred to. Did it mean young? But why the red skin? Were they some advancement in potato technology, along the lines of NASA's replacement of oranges with Tang™?*

This recipe goes one better than Mom's by roasting the smashed gems and brushing them with duck fat (or butter, if you have a soft spot for Daffy). Duck fat is often available at a grocer or online at D'Artagnan, but if you have made the Duck Breast with Fig-Orange Sauce on page 102, you will have saved the rendered fat for just this moment.

EVIE • *I have a soft spot for Daffy, and this is fantastic with butter.*

Makes 4 servings

1½ pounds red new potatoes (about 20)

Melted duck fat or butter

Salt

Freshly ground pepper

Garlic powder or garlic salt

Heat the oven to 400°F with a rack in the center position. Boil the potatoes in plenty of salted water until they are easily pierced with a fork.

Drain the potatoes and place the still-hot potatoes on a paper towel–lined baking sheet. Then smash them with whatever suits you. Press down until the potatoes are about ½ inch thick but still in one piece. Take the paper towels off the baking sheet and brush the potatoes with melted duck fat that you cleverly saved or melted butter. Sprinkle with salt, pepper, and garlic powder (or garlic salt, which does both, I suppose), and pop into the oven. Bake for 30 minutes, or until the skin is crisp. If you've done it right—i.e., if I've explained it right—the potatoes should be crunchy with a creamy center.

CAULIFLOWER PUREE

STEPHEN • *As I said in the Chickpea Fries recipe (page 52), I once fell prey to the no-carb cult. For seven months, I dreamt up new ways to fool my carb cravings, and this is the recipe that I kept up even when taters were back on the menu. The steamed cauliflower (something I don't associate with flavor) transforms into a smooth, creamy, and savory side dish that is also vegan. Self-deception has never been so satisfying.*

EVIE • *I know cauliflower rice is really a thing now, but this is really cauliflower mashed potatoes, and it does not disappoint.*

**Makes about 5 cups;
4 to 6 servings**

**1 head of cauliflower
(about 1½ pounds)**

6 cloves garlic

**¼ cup extra-virgin olive oil,
plus more as needed, for
garnish**

**Salt and freshly ground
pepper**

**2 tablespoons chopped
fresh chives, for garnish**

You'll need a steamer setup of some kind—the (inexpensive) collapsible type that fits into a pot or a serious steamer-in-a-pot combo. Either, or anything in between, will do.

Pull off the green leaves from the cauliflower and cut off the end of the stem. Cut the cauliflower into 3-inch chunks. Steam the chunks over water at a rolling boil until you can pierce them easily with a paring knife, about 15 minutes. Make sure the pot lid is tightly closed while the cauliflower is steaming.

Meanwhile, roughly slice the garlic. Heat the olive oil and sliced garlic in a small skillet over medium-low heat. Keep the temperature fairly low, as garlic burns easily. As soon as it shows any color, take it off the heat right away.

Place the hot, steamed cauliflower in a food processor, add the garlic and oil, and blend until smooth. You may want to add a bit more olive oil to loosen the mix. Add salt and pepper to taste. You can serve the cauliflower immediately or return it to the pot to keep warm over very low heat.

Garnish with an extra drizzle of olive oil and a sprinkle of the chives.

HOPPIN' JOHN

STEPHEN • *As a struggling actor, I ate my weight in rice and beans cooked many ways, but Hoppin' John is the best—if you hit it with a little hot sauce at the table. Evie does not approve. "We're from Charleston, not New Orleans." True, but I am willing to betray our hometown for flavor.*

EVIE • *This is yet another classic Southern dish that owes its origins to West Africa. It is a Charleston tradition that eating Hoppin' John and collard greens on New Year's Day will bring you a year of good luck. That belief was so drilled into me growing up that once I left Charleston, I continued to make Hoppin' John every New Year's Day. And yes, this is a typical Charleston-style dish, heavy on the bacon grease and light on the hot sauce. (But go ahead and add some if you want; it won't dilute the good luck!)*

*
pictured on
pages 200–201

Makes 8 servings

4 slices bacon, cut crosswise into 1-inch-wide strips

1 medium onion, chopped

1 cup dried field peas or dried black-eyed peas

1 teaspoon salt, or to taste

1 cup long-grain white rice

tip—Some peas will cook faster than others: 45 minutes to 1½ hours is a good basic guide. If the water level dips below the top of the peas before they are tender, pour in enough water to cover them by about 2 inches and keep on cooking.

Put the bacon in a 2-quart saucepan (tall and narrow is better than short and wide) and cook over medium-high heat until the bacon has rendered a lot of fat and is light brown. Stir in the onion and continue cooking for a few minutes, until softened. Add the field peas and enough water to cover by about 3 inches. Bring to a boil, then adjust the heat to a lively simmer and cook, uncovered, until the peas are tender, about 50 minutes (see Tip).

Drain the peas, reserving the liquid. Cook the rice according to the package directions, using some or all of the pea cooking liquid in place of the water called for in the rice instructions.

When the rice is done, stir in the cooked peas and check the seasoning. Spoon the Hoppin' John into bowls and serve with collards (page 204)—mandatory on New Year's Day, optional at other times.

198 *Does This Taste Funny?*

SCALLOPED POTATOES

STEPHEN • *Though the potato is native to the Incas, the Irish took spuds to heart. I don't want to know what organ the French took it to, but they achieved another level of pomme de terre perfection. This dish has a savory richness that will roll your eyes back in your skull. They are more than gastronomic. They are narcotic. They border on the erotic.*

EVIE • *These scalloped potatoes are really quick and easy to make. They are an excellent side dish with a pork tenderloin or steak au poivre. The thinly sliced potatoes soften up nicely so you can eat this easily with just a spoon. If you have a mandoline slicer, now is the time to use it (carefully). If not, aim for nice, even slices. But truthfully, once the potatoes are slathered in cream, topped with cheese, and baked until bubbly, a little uneven knife work won't really show.*

✳
pictured on
pages 200–201

Makes 8 to 10 servings

1 tablespoon olive oil

4 cloves garlic

4 to 5 russet potatoes
(about 2½ pounds), peeled
(see Note)

Salt and freshly ground
pepper

10 ounces Gruyère cheese,
shredded (about 3 lightly
packed cups)

1 cup heavy cream

Very thinly sliced garlic
makes this dish. Smallish
inexpensive mandolines,
like those made by Benriner,
are perfect for the task. Nice
to have, not essential.

Heat the oven to 350°F with a rack in the upper position. Lightly coat an 8 × 11-inch baking dish with the olive oil. Slice the garlic cloves like Paulie did in *Goodfellas*—i.e., super-thin. Paulie used a razor blade, you can use a Japanese mini-mandoline. If you don't own one, just slice the cloves as thin as you can.

Slice the potatoes very thin (about ⅛ inch). Shingle about one-third of the potatoes over the bottom of the baking dish. Season with salt and pepper. Top with one-third of the cheese and one-third of the cream. Scatter some of the thinly sliced garlic over the cream. Repeat to make two more layers.

Bake until the potatoes are fork-tender and the cheese is golden brown on top, about 1 hour. Let stand for 5 to 10 minutes before serving—that will make the potatoes easier to cut into squares.

NOTE

• The potatoes can be peeled up to several hours in advance. Put them in a bowl, cover completely with cold water to prevent them from turning brown, and keep them in the fridge until you are ready to put together the casserole. Wait until just before building the casserole to slice them. If you're a slow slicer (no judgment), you may want to put the slices in a bowl of cool water as you slice them. Drain thoroughly before assembling the casserole.

Jim's SPAGHETTI SQUASH CASSEROLE

STEPHEN • *When I was a young actor panning for gold in Los Angeles, I would live with my brother Jim and his wife, Vicki. Jim is a great cook and a great storyteller with a great wine cellar. I have so many happy memories of sitting at his counter watching him whip up something fantastic, stirring the pan with one hand, gripping a glass with the other, and making me laugh. My siblings are all funnier than I am. Just ask them.*

✳ pictured on pages 200–201

JIM COLBERT • *This is an easy-to-prepare vegetarian main dish that can also be served as a side dish with grilled meat or fish. After cooking, the flesh will come out of the "shell" in long, thin strings resembling spaghetti (which gives the squash its name). Discard the skin.*

Makes 2 main-course or 4 side-dish servings

1 medium spaghetti squash (about 2½ pounds)

1 tablespoon extra-virgin olive oil, or as needed

1 medium onion, diced

2 cups diced tomatoes (fresh, Pomì brand in the carton, or canned)

¼ cup chopped fresh basil

1 cup grated Parmesan cheese (preferably Parmigiano-Reggiano)

Cut off the stem end of the squash. Stand the squash cut side down on a cutting board and cut it lengthwise in two. Scoop out and discard the seeds.

Fill a microwave-safe dish with water to a depth of ¼ to ½ inch. (A 13 × 11-inch baking dish works well.) Put the squash halves cut side down in the dish. Microwave on high until you can easily pierce the skin with a table fork, about 20 minutes. Let cool while you make the sauce.

Heat the oil in a large nonstick skillet (use a little more oil if your skillet is not nonstick) over very low heat. Stir in the onions and cook until soft and translucent, about 10 minutes. Do not let the onions turn brown or become crisp. Add the tomatoes and basil and continue cooking until warm. (If using fresh tomatoes, cook a little longer, just until soft.) Remove from the heat.

Heat the oven to 350°F. Using a table fork, strip the "spaghetti" from the squash halves into a large bowl. Add the tomato sauce and ½ cup of the grated Parmesan and toss gently until well mixed. Carefully scrape the spaghetti into an oiled 11-inch oval (or similar size) casserole/baking dish. Sprinkle the remaining ½ cup Parmesan over the top.

Cover and bake for 25 to 30 minutes.

Crispy Hot-Honey
BRUSSELS SPROUTS

EVIE • *Our nephews Joe and Theo Wichmann shared this receipt with us. Like everyone else in the Wichmann family, both boys are great cooks. In an act of brotherly love or rivalry—I am not sure which—Joe and Theo worked together to write up this receipt for us. We love it. The crispiness of the Brussels sprouts really works here.*

✳ pictured on pages 200–201

STEPHEN • *If, like me, you grew up with damp, bitter Brussels sprouts one night a year, you know how strange it is that these mini cabbages have become so popular. Why? Well, recipes like this one have changed the game, but it turns out the sprouts have changed too. Starting in the '90s, crossbreeding by the Dutch (who also gave us orange carrots, btw) eliminated most of the bitter taste we remember. Can the Dutch fix collards next?* Alstublieft!

Makes 4 to 6 servings

1½ pounds Brussels sprouts, ends trimmed and cut in half through the core

¼ cup olive oil, or a little more if needed

5 cloves garlic, minced or grated

2 teaspoons salt

1 teaspoon freshly ground pepper

2 tablespoons unsalted butter

1 tablespoon hot honey or regular honey plus a healthy pinch of red pepper flakes

variations

• Cook some diced pancetta in the pan before adding the sprouts.

• Top with truffle honey instead of hot honey.

Toss the Brussels sprouts, 2 tablespoons of the olive oil, ⅔ of the minced garlic, the salt, and the pepper together in a large bowl. Mix thoroughly and let stand for 15 minutes.

In a large skillet, preferably cast iron, heat the remaining 2 tablespoons olive oil over medium-high heat. Keep an eye on it, and as soon as it begins to smoke a little, start slipping the sprouts into the pan, cut side down. Get in as many as you can without crowding them, and lower the heat slightly, to medium. Cook until the undersides are deep golden brown, about 4 minutes. Remove the sprouts to a bowl. If there isn't enough oil in the pan to cook the second round of sprouts, pour in a little more. Repeat the browning with the remaining sprouts.

Add the first batch of sprouts to those in the pan. Toss them around and cook for another 2 or 3 minutes to cook off some of the excess moisture and encourage crispiness. Add the remaining minced garlic and the butter to the pan and, using a wooden spatula, scrape up the fond (French for gunk) you've created on the bottom of the pan.

Spoon the sprouts into a serving bowl (you can even put them back in that original mixing bowl) and drizzle with the hot honey.

Claus's COLLARD GREENS

STEPHEN • *This recipe is included at Evie's insistence. I am not a fan. Too many servings in elementary school of this leathery leaf that had been boiled from hell to breakfast. But Evie says we can't include Hoppin' John (page 198) if we don't have collards. Something about messing with the good luck. I am calling BS, because we have Hoppin' John every New Year's (even on vacation, she will hunt down some form of rice and beans), but I don't remember a lot of collards. What do you have to say to that, darling?*

EVIE • *Hush up! Collards go with Hoppin' John the way champagne goes with New Year's Eve. We eat the rice and beans on New Year's Day to soak up the effects of the champagne from the night before, but without the collards, we aren't getting the tanginess needed to start off the year with some zip and zing.*

STEPHEN • *I apologize.*

Makes about 8 cups; 8 servings

4 to 5 bunches collard greens
(3½ to 4 pounds)

1 tablespoon unsalted butter

1 tablespoon olive oil

4 to 5 slices bacon, cut
crosswise into ½-inch-wide
pieces

½ cup shredded smoked ham,
leftover from a dinner ham or
from a store-bought ham steak

1 sweet onion, such as Vidalia,
thinly sliced

2 tablespoons sugar

One 12-ounce bottle or can of
beer, or more if needed

Salt and freshly ground
pepper

**FOR PASSING AT THE TABLE
(OPTIONAL)**

Apple cider vinegar

Texas Pete hot sauce or other
hot sauce

> You'll need a very large, as
> in 8- to 9-quart, pot to hold
> all the collards.

Cut or strip the stems from the collards (see the sidebar). Cut
the leaves into strips about 1½ inches wide. Wash the collards
thoroughly to remove all dirt; this is best done in a sink full of cool
water. Drain them well.

Heat the butter and olive oil in a large, heavy pot over medium
heat (an 8- to 9-quart Dutch oven or similar pot works well).
When the butter is melted, stir in the bacon, ham, and onion.
Cook, stirring occasionally, until the bacon is lightly browned,
about 10 minutes. Remove the pot from the heat and scoop the
bacon-ham-onion mix into a bowl.

Make an even layer in the bottom of the pot with about one-
quarter of the collards. Top with about one-quarter of the bacon-
ham-onion mix and sprinkle some of the sugar over it. Repeat
three times to fill the pot. Pour the beer over the collards. Bring to
a boil over medium heat, reduce the heat to a simmer, and cover
the pot. Simmer until the collards are very tender, anywhere from
2½ to 4 hours. The first time you check the collards (at around
the 2-hour mark), add salt and pepper if you think it's needed. If
the collards seem too dry and start to stick, add additional beer as
needed.

Spoon the collards and some of the pot likker into bowls. Pass
the vinegar and hot sauce, if you like, at the table.

STRIPPING STEMS FROM COLLARDS (AND OTHER HEARTY GREENS)

Sure, you can cut the stems from collards with
a knife, but here's a little shortcut: Hold the end
of the stem of a collard in one hand and make
the OK sign with the thumb and forefinger of
your other hand. Starting at the stem end, run
the OK sign along the stem to separate it from
the leaves. Repeat with the remaining greens,
discarding the stems, and prep the leaves as
called for in the recipe. (This works with chard,
kale, and other sturdy leafy greens as well.)

WILD RICE
with Cranberries and Toasted Almonds

EVIE • *We have this dish every Christmas and Thanksgiving. To me, wild rice is so special and rare, it feels right for the holidays. I adapted this years ago from a receipt in* Jane Brody's Good Food Book. *I like the tanginess of the cranberries and the crispness of the almonds, but you could also use Jane's original currants and pine nuts.*

STEPHEN • *Every Thanksgiving and Christmas, Evie says, "Maybe I shouldn't do the wild rice this year. I'm not sure if people like it." I don't know who these "people" are. She likes it. I like it. The kids like it. The people have spoken, Ev.*

Makes about 6 cups; 10 servings

2 cups vegetable or chicken broth, homemade or store-bought

1 cup water

½ pound wild rice (about 1½ cups)

½ cup dried cranberries

1 teaspoon salt, or as needed

Freshly ground pepper

½ cup slivered almonds

4 tablespoons (½ stick) butter or, to make this a vegan dish, margarine or canola oil

1 medium onion, finely chopped (about 1½ cups)

Bring the broth and water to a boil in a 3-quart saucepan. Add the wild rice, cranberries, salt, and a couple good grinds of pepper, reduce the heat to low, cover the pan, and simmer until the liquid is absorbed and the rice is tender, about 1 hour. Keep an eye on the rice: if the liquid is gone before the rice is tender, add a little more water. Or, if there is liquid left when the rice is tender, turn up the heat and cook it off. Remove from the heat.

Meanwhile, toast the almonds in a small skillet over low heat; be sure to toss them frequently so they don't burn. Set aside. In the same skillet, heat the butter. Add the onion, season lightly with salt, and sauté until translucent but with a little bite, about 10 minutes.

Toss the finished rice with the onion and almonds and serve.

NOTES

• This is the perfect dish to make ahead of time. Cook the rice and onion and toast the almonds, but keep them separate. Just before serving, toss everything together in a large bowl and reheat.

• The best way to see if the wild rice is tender is to test it from time to time. The brand of rice you're using and how long ago it was harvested will affect the cooking time.

Buttermilk
CORNBREAD

EVIE • *This cornbread is adapted from a receipt I found in my grandmother's receipt box. We make it in a cast-iron skillet just the way I suspect she did. The buttermilk adds the perfect amount of tangy sweetness.*

STEPHEN • *In the Old South, biscuits and cornbread were markers of status. Biscuits needed folding and beating. That's for people with time on their hands or help in the house. Cornbread is mixed, poured, and cooked—so easy, so cheap, and so good. Man of the people that I am, I will take a fresh piece of cornbread over a biscuit any day.*

Makes 8 servings

2 tablespoons unsalted butter, plus 4 tablespoons (½ stick), melted and cooled

2 cups fine yellow cornmeal

½ cup all-purpose flour

2 tablespoons sugar

2 teaspoons baking powder

1 teaspoon baking soda

1 teaspoon salt

1¼ cups buttermilk

2 large eggs

> You'll need a 9-inch cast-iron skillet to make this authentic version with a firm, golden brown crust.

Heat the oven to 400°F with a rack in the center position. Start melting the 2 tablespoons butter in a 9-inch cast-iron skillet over very low heat.

Meanwhile, whisk the cornmeal, flour, sugar, baking powder, baking soda, and salt in a large bowl until blended. In a separate medium bowl, whisk the buttermilk, the 4 tablespoons melted butter, and the eggs together until thoroughly blended. Stir the wet ingredients into the dry just until blended—a few lumps are OK.

Turn up the heat under the skillet to medium. When the butter stops foaming and just begins to take on color in places, pour in the batter. Shake the pan to smooth the top and put the skillet into the oven. Bake until the cornbread is golden around the edges with a few cracks in the center, about 25 minutes. The center should feel springy when you press it lightly.

Cool the cornbread on a wire rack for about 30 minutes before cutting and serving. Be careful! The skillet will remain hot for a while. No one will mind if you serve this with room-temp butter or, for breakfast, butter whipped with Fig Preserves (page 280) or maple syrup (see Fun with Muffins, page 271).

Lulu's Johns Island
TOMATO SHED PIE

EVIE • *Stephen's sister Lulu has been bringing this tomato pie to our 4th of July parties for as long as I can remember. It's so delicious, and honestly, it wouldn't feel like the 4th if I didn't have a slice of Lulu's tomato pie. Of course, locally grown ripe tomatoes are the best, but if you don't have those, you can substitute Romas or heirlooms or even cherry tomatoes from the grocery store.*

STEPHEN • *I love that Lulu brings this pie to the 4th of July party every year, because I remember when she and Margo worked in the Johns Island tomato sheds. The men picked in the fields and the women sorted in the sheds. At home, she used to imitate the yelled instructions of the foreman: "Tighten up on them wormholes, girls!"*

½ recipe All-Purpose
Food Processor Pie Pastry
(page 232)

2 ripe medium tomatoes,
or 4 medium Roma (plum)
tomatoes or ¾ pound
heirlooms

Salt

1½ cups shredded
sharp cheddar cheese
(4 to 5 ounces)

1 cup mayonnaise

8 large fresh basil leaves

½ cup thinly sliced green
onions

Freshly ground pepper

Roll out the chilled dough, fit it into a 9-inch pie pan (see Note), and chill it, then blind-bake, all according to the directions in the pastry recipe (page 233). Let cool completely.

Line a baking sheet with a double thickness of paper towels. Core the tomatoes and cut them in half through the equator. Gently but firmly squeeze out as many seeds (and the liquid that comes along with them) as you can. Cut the squeezed tomatoes into ½-inch pieces and spread them out on the paper towels. Sprinkle them lightly with salt and set aside for about an hour. (Salting the tomatoes helps to draw out a bit of their moisture and prevent a soggy piecrust.)

Heat the oven to 375°F with a rack in the lowest position. Stir the cheese and mayonnaise together in a small bowl until blended.

Dollop a small amount of the cheesy mayo into the bottom of the cooled shell and smear with the back of a spoon to coat the bottom of it lightly but evenly. If necessary, dollop in a little more mayo mix to finish up the job.

Blot the tomatoes dry and scatter them evenly over the mayo. Scatter the green onions and basil over the tomatoes. Season with pepper. Dollop the remaining mayo mix evenly over the tomatoes and, using the back of a spoon dipped in water, smooth the mayo mix into an even layer; re-dip the spoon often. Most likely, some of the basil and green onions will poke their way up through the top—not to worry.

Bake until the topping is light brown and the edges of the filling are bubbling, about 30 minutes. Let cool for 20 to 30 minutes before slicing and serving.

NOTE

• Many pie plates today are very deep. For this and the other pies and tarts in this book, choose a pie plate no more than 1½ inches deep.

Sourdough
BREAD

EVIE • *Luckily for us, in the fall of 2020, our youngest child, John, decided to take a gap year before heading off to college. Since the world was still largely shut down, John was stuck at home with us. I'm sure it was not his first choice, but we loved having him around. He spent a lot of his time either playing his guitar and singing or baking bread. It was like living in a bakery with live entertainment. John shares his bread-baking tips here. You will have to ask him directly for his guitar-playing tips.*

JOHN • *After I graduated high school in June of 2020, I decided, due to some unnamed circumstances that arose around that time, to take a year off before going to college. I found myself with disturbingly little to do. I needed to eat food, so that was something. But then I realized, if I have to eat food, that food needs to get cooked. I could cook it! Suddenly I had purpose. But what to cook? "I like bread," I thought. And there I had it. Now I just had to figure out how to make it.*

Thankfully, most of America seemingly was thinking the same thing, because the internet was bursting with blogs itching to teach aspiring bakers how to make sourdough bread. So, I read them, and I ended up with this recipe, a mixture of a few different techniques that made the most sense to me. I would encourage playing around with this recipe, if you want. Keep in mind that the strength and flavor of your starter will be slightly different, depending on where you are, since the yeast and bacteria come from the air around you. Also, the moisture and temperature of your home will affect how the dough rises, so if this recipe doesn't turn out how you want, don't worry about it, and try to adjust things. Making bread is fun because it has a mind of its own. Think of it like a soft, vulnerable friend who, though they're pretty dumb, will do what you want if you treat them with care.

Also, many websites will tell you not to cut into your bread until it's cool so that it continues to cook after you remove it from the oven. I did this for a long time, but I don't think it's worth giving up the joy of warm bread.

This bread is best eaten all at once, since it can go stale fast, so feel no shame about eating half the loaf yourself.

continued $\longrightarrow$

Makes 2 loaves

> You will have the best results if you use a kitchen scale for the starter and the bread recipe.

THE STARTER

Creating a starter that is healthy, is active, and imparts a full, pleasantly sour flavor to bread is a blend of art and science. Temperature, humidity, and the amount of wild yeast and beneficial bacteria present in the air and in your flour all contribute to make each starter experience just a little bit different. We tried a few approaches but finally settled on a mash-up of the process from *Tartine Bread* (as photographed by our very own Eric Wolfinger!) and Maurizio Leo's The Perfect Loaf website.

The best advice we can offer is to remember that time alone doesn't determine when to feed a starter or when to add the starter to a bread dough. Let your eyes and nose be your guide. And be patient—you could be looking at a two-week babysitting job before your baby—i.e., your starter—is ready to roll.

Get started: Make a mix of equal parts of whole wheat and white flour (either all-purpose or bread flour)—about 400 grams of each is a good start—and set this aside. This is the mix you'll be using to feed the starter. Choose a clear glass jar with fairly straight sides and a lid. A 1-quart Weck canning jar is a good choice. Weigh the jar and make a note of the weight.

Make the first mix: Pick a time of day that is convenient for you to feed the starter for the next week or two. An hour either way doesn't matter in the long run, but consistency helps. Mornings are good, because you will eventually need to add another feeding later in the day. In the glass jar, stir together 100 grams of the flour mix and 125 grams room-temperature water. Mix well, but don't worry about getting rid of all lumps. Put the jar on a small baking sheet, cover loosely with the lid, and set the jar in a warm place. A turned-off oven with the light on is a good starting option.

• If you're preparing your starter in the winter in a cool, dry house, try leaving it on your bathroom counter. The steam from showers will help the starter develop. And goose the starter a little by using lukewarm water for the starter feedings.

• If you're unsure if your starter is ready, you can perform something called the "float test" by dropping a pinch (1 teaspoon or so) of the starter into a bowl of cool water. If it floats, it's ready; if it sinks, allow it to rest a little longer, repeating this test every 30 minutes until it floats.

Feeding: About 24 hours after you made the first mix, it's time to start the once-a-day feedings. Scrape out and discard all but 75 grams of the flour/water mix: Put the jar on the scale and figure out the weight of the glass jar + 75 grams—that's why you weighed the jar! Add 100 grams each of the flour mix and room-temperature water and stir to mix. Clean up the sides of the jar, replace the lid, and return the jar to a warm spot. (Don't be surprised if the starter has a "growth spurt" on Day 2. Encouraging, but that probably won't be the case every day after feeding.) Repeat this process of discarding/feeding, using the same amounts given above, on Days 3 and 4. You should start to see some activity—this is a good sign, but not the end of the sourdough road. The starter will have to show signs of activity and a (more or less) steady schedule of bubbling, rising, and falling before it's ready to use in a loaf. On the evening of Day 4, begin twice-a-day feedings, repeating the same process in the evenings as you did in the morning.

Evaluating and regular feeding: By the morning of Day 5, you should see increasing signs of activity in your starter on a somewhat regular schedule: it will show large bubbles around the sides of the jar with some bubbling on the top as well. The level of starter will rise in the jar, sometimes doubling in height, sometimes a little more or less, before beginning to collapse. The aroma should be pleasantly sour, like sour cream or yogurt, not like vinegar. Just when the bubbling activity slows and the starter begins to lose height is the best time to feed it. You'll get more in tune with the way the starter behaves the longer you keep at it. Remember, this kind of regular activity and the rising and falling that go along with it are entirely dependent on your situation. Some starters might fall into this pattern after 5 or 6 days, and others may take up to 2 weeks. When you notice a string of several days when the starter looks healthy, begins to rise and fall regularly, and smells wonderful, you're ready to bake.

continued ⟶

THE BREAD

1000 grams high-quality white bread flour, plus more for dusting the work surfaces

750 grams lukewarm water

200 grams sourdough starter

20 grams salt

The morning of your sourdough journey, start by feeding the starter with the discard-and-replace method above. The starter will be ready to use when it's bubbly and nearly doubled in size.

Beginning with a step called "autolyse," combine the bread flour with 725 grams of the lukewarm water in a large bowl and mix until the flour is hydrated. Be careful not to overmix. Cover with a damp kitchen towel and let this mixture rest on the countertop for 30 minutes to an hour.

With your ripe, bubbly fresh starter, begin the second phase of bread making. Add the 200 grams starter, the remaining 25 grams water, and the salt to the rested flour/water mixture. Mix to combine well, with either your hands or a plastic bench scraper. (Hands are messy but ultimately easier.) The mixture will be very sticky. Cover with a damp towel and let sit for 10 minutes.

Once the dough has rested, use a wet hand to reach into the bowl and "fold" the dough by pulling it up from the bottom and stretching that handful up onto the top of the dough. Rotate the bowl 90 degrees and do the same. Repeat about ten times, turning the bowl a quarter-turn after each fold. Transfer the mixture to a clean bowl, cover with a damp towel, and let rest for its "bulk fermentation" in a warm place for about 60 minutes. A turned-off oven with the light turned on works well for this, as it did for the starter.

After it has rested, uncover the dough and repeat the stretching and folding technique four times, rotating the bowl a quarter-turn after each fold. (This is one "turn.") Let the dough rest for 30 minutes, then give the dough 3 to 4 turns, letting it rest for 30 minutes after each turn. By the end of bulk fermentation, the dough should be light, pillowy, and increased in size. If the dough doesn't look like that, let it rest in its warm place until it does.

Turn out the dough onto a lightly floured work surface and, using a bench scraper, divide it in half. Keep the two mounds of dough separated—they like to try and merge back together if left to their own devices. Using your hands, guide one piece of dough into a neat and tidy round loaf. One way to do this: Hold your hands like parentheses on opposite sides of the dough, pull the dough out from the sides, and tuck under the dough blob.

Continue, rotating the dough after each tuck, until you have a smooth ball with a taut surface. Repeat with the remaining half of the dough.

Once both loaves are shaped, cover them with a damp kitchen towel and let rest for 20 minutes while you prepare the dough baskets. You can use two bread proofing bowls or *bannetons* (designed for just this purpose), or two medium-large colanders. Line each one with a clean, dry kitchen towel that has been well dusted with flour. Flip your rested dough gently into the baskets, bottom side up. Lightly dust the exposed side with flour and cover with a dry kitchen towel. Let rest on the counter for 1 to 1½ hours. The dough should increase slightly in volume and pass the "poke test"—when it is gently poked, it should hold your finger imprint and slowly spring back. If the dough springs back quickly when poked, it needs more time to rest.

Once the dough passes the poke test, remove the covering towels, cover the proofing baskets or colanders with plastic wrap, and put them in the fridge for at least 6 to 8 hours, or up to overnight.

When ready to bake, remove one of the loaves and let it come to room temperature. Meanwhile, put a 4- to 5-quart Dutch oven (with the lid) in the middle rack of the oven and turn the oven to 450°F, so the pot preheats along with the oven.

Gently turn the dough from the basket onto a piece of parchment paper on the counter. Score it deeply with a razor blade, sharp knife, or lame (bread blade), creating a cut from one side of the dough to the other.

Open the preheated oven, pull out the rack with the Dutch oven, and, working quickly and carefully, transfer the dough, still on the parchment to the hot pot. Cover with the lid. Bake for 20 minutes, then remove the lid and bake for another 45 minutes, or until the loaf is deep golden brown.

Remove the pot from the oven and, working carefully, use the parchment paper to lift the bread onto a cooling rack. While the first loaf is cooling, bake the second loaf, making sure the Dutch oven is fully preheated. Let the bread cool for 2 hours before slicing it. Serve it with many things—salted butter, or jams, or a fried egg, or . . .

Au·tol·y·sis, according to the *Merriam-Webster* dictionary, is the "breakdown of all or part of a cell or tissue by self-produced enzymes." Or in regular person speak: letting the mix of flour and water sit for an hour or two creates the gluten needed for a successful loaf of bread. This is the same type of gluten produced by prolonged kneading in traditional bread recipes.

RHUBARB
(OR ANY FRUIT,
REALLY) CRISP
224

ALMOND-PEAR
GALETTE
226

CHESS PIE
231

ALL-PURPOSE
FOOD PROCESSOR
PIE PASTRY
232

MRS. McGEE'S
BOURBON
CHOCOLATE
PECAN PIE
234

FIG TARTS
FOR INA
237

HUGUENOT
TORTE
238

ANOTHER
CARROT CAKE
241

STEPHEN
CANDIES SOME
TANGERINE RIND
244

STICKY TOFFEE
PUDDING
247

CARA'S
ALMOND-BASIL
COOKIES
249

KEY LIME PIE
250

THE COLBERT
FUDGE
SIBLING SAGA
253

FUDGY
BROWNIES
257

DESSERTS

At the end of a dinner party, it's always fun to yell, "No one move. There's dessert!" And then to hear, "Oh no, I couldn't." And then to see that, oh yes, they can.

This is one of the longer chapters in the book, so apparently, we're big on dessert. Of course, we love sugar and butter in all its seductive forms, but Evie reminds me that desserts are also a great way to postpone cleaning up. And what constitutes a dessert is flexible. While there are some lovely recipes to follow, our family doesn't need the perfect tart to stay at the table. At our house, there's usually a pint of Americone Dream to dig out of the freezer or a few hunks of good cheese ("We should probably open one more bottle, yes?") or just a nice plate of cookies in the center of the table to keep the conversation going and (to paraphrase Tolkien) to keep the company in that tolerant and delightful stage called "filling up the corners."

Some of these desserts are very old family recipes and some are very new family recipes and some are very good recipes borrowed from very good friends we have made sitting around that table.

And if your dinner party goes so well that your friends stay the night, the fig tarts (page 237) and the almond-pear galette (page 226) make a great breakfast. • **STEPHEN**

RHUBARB
(or Any Fruit, Really)
CRISP

EVIE • *I love a good rhubarb crisp, and this one is the best going. After our first child was born, a friend brought me this dish as a gift. It might be because I had just given birth and was still in some sort of postpartum haze, but it was the most delicious thing I had ever eaten, and I still think about it nearly twenty-eight years later! I hope you will have a similar euphoric experience.*

STEPHEN • *This is all I know about rhubarb:*
- *It's a weird word. That "h" after an "r" is pretty rare. Rhythm Rhyme Rhombus Rhizome Rhubarb . . .*
- *My dad loved rhubarb.*
- *The Joker advises us: "Never rub another man's rhubarb."*
- *The next time Evie has a baby, I gotta remember to make this!*

Makes 12 servings

THE FRUIT

6 cups trimmed and sliced (½-inch-thick) rhubarb (see the sidebar), approximately 2 pounds

¾ to 1 cup granulated sugar

3 tablespoons cornstarch

THE TOPPING

2 cups old-fashioned (not instant) oats

½ pound (2 sticks) unsalted butter, melted and cooled

1 cup all-purpose flour

¾ cup packed light brown sugar

Heat the oven to 350°F with a rack in the upper third of the oven.

Prepare the fruit: Toss the rhubarb, ¾ cup of the sugar, and the cornstarch together in a medium bowl. Let stand, tossing a few times, until the rhubarb gives up its juices and the sugar is dissolved. Taste the syrup and add more sugar if you think it needs it. Scrape the fruit and syrup into a 13 × 9-inch (or similar size) baking dish.

Make the topping: In a medium bowl, mush the oats, melted butter, flour, and brown sugar together with your fingertips until everything is evenly mixed. Crumble the topping evenly over the fruit.

Bake until the topping is golden and the edges are bubbling slightly, about 45 minutes. Let the crisp cool for at least half an hour before serving. It's absolutely delicious warm or at room temperature.

FRUIT CRISP BLUEPRINT

A delicious crisp can be made with just about any fruit. A few guidelines: Start with ripe fruit! Cut—or don't cut—the fruit into pieces, depending on which fruit you're using: e.g., peaches, plums, or apricots in thin slices, large strawberries halved, blueberries and blackberries right out of the basket. You'll need a compact 6 cups of cut-up fruit. Start with the lesser amount of sugar in the recipe. After the fruit has been sitting a little bit, taste the syrup. If it seems a little tart, add more sugar. And some fruits will require more cornstarch than others. A good rule of thumb is to use a little more cornstarch than what is listed in the recipe for juicier fruits like berries and ripe peaches. Fillings made with sturdier ingredients, like apricots and rhubarb, need less thickening because they have less juice. When in doubt, less cornstarch is the safer bet. You can always serve a juicier crisp in bowls instead of on plates.

Almond-Pear
GALETTE

EVIE • *Every so often Stephen will go on a cooking binge (this frequently happens when he is avoiding doing some other project, like writing a script or preparing for an appearance). He created this incredibly delicious dessert one Saturday afternoon and then had the audacity to say he wasn't going to eat any! So I ate enough for both of us.*

STEPHEN • *Almonds are tasty, and almond paste is tasty, but almond paste doesn't taste like almonds. It's a mystery. I had fantasized about this tart for years (I have a rich inner life) before buckling down to make it.*

Evie's right—I do cook when I'm avoiding working on a project. But when the project is a cookbook, that doesn't work!

Makes 16 servings

THE PEARS

6 very firm pears

4 tablespoons (½ stick) unsalted butter

½ cup granulated sugar

THE FRANGIPANE

10 tablespoons (1¼ sticks) unsalted butter, at room temperature

¾ cup granulated sugar

3 large eggs

½ teaspoon almond extract

1¼ cups almond flour (aka almond meal), sifted

¼ cup all-purpose flour, sifted

Make the pear filling: Peel and core the pears, then cut each one lengthwise into 8 wedges. Melt the butter in a large skillet over medium heat, then add the pears. Sprinkle with the sugar and stir. Cook until the pears release their liquid and make a clear syrup. Turn the heat up to medium-high and cook, stirring occasionally, to tighten up the syrup a little.

Turn the heat up to high and cook, stirring frequently to keep them from burning, until the pears turn a light brown and the syrup begins to caramelize, about 15 minutes. Take the pears off the heat and let cool.

While the pears are cooling, make the frangipane: In the bowl of a stand mixer fitted with the paddle attachment, or in a large bowl using a handheld mixer, beat the softened butter with the sugar until airy. Then add the eggs one at a time, scraping the bowl after each addition. Add the almond extract. Sift the almond flour through a coarse sieve to lighten it and add it in heaping spoonfuls to the egg-sugar mixture. Finally, mix in the all-purpose flour on low speed. The frangipane should be soft but not liquid, and very spreadable.

recipe and ingredients continued $\longrightarrow$

About ⅔ package filo pastry (10 to 12 sheets)

Melted butter as needed (about 8 tablespoons [1 stick])

2 tablespoons cognac or other brandy or bourbon

2 tablespoons granulated sugar

2 tablespoons butter

Pinch of salt

1 cup very cold heavy cream

1 tablespoon confectioners' sugar

¼ teaspoon almond extract

tip—Be very careful when working with sugar syrups like this caramel or the fudge on pages 255–56. Make sure the pan or pot is always steady on the burner and handle the finished syrup slowly. You may even want to throw on a long-sleeved shirt and silicone gloves or oven mitts.

Heat the oven to 400°F with a rack in the center position.

Make the crust: Unfold the filo pastry on the countertop and cover with a clean, damp kitchen towel to keep it from drying out. Line a baking sheet with a silicone mat or parchment paper and lay out one sheet of the filo lengthwise in the pan. Brush with melted butter, then lay another filo sheet across it, perpendicular to the first, and butter it. Continue, alternating the direction of the layers and buttering each one, until you have 10 to 12 layers. I do 12, and it seems good. Experiment.

When all the layers are in place, spread the frangipane into a large circle in the center of the filo. The frangipane should almost cover the area where the filo layers overlap—leave some space between the frangipane and the "corners" where the sheets of filo intersect. This frangipane puddle will be essentially the size of your tart. You don't need to use all the frangipane. I usually use about three-quarters, but to each his own.

Next, fold the "corner" intersections of the filo inward over the edges of the frangipane, so the soon-to-be galette is an octagonal shape: Go all around the tart, folding the edges of the filo in over the edges of the frangipane, until you are "containing" the frangipane.

Take the somewhat cooled (but probably still warm) pears and arrange them in a pattern you find pleasing. (Don't wash the pear pan just yet.) Bake until the pastry is a deep golden brown and the frangipane is browning as well, about 22 minutes.

While the galette is cooking, make the caramel: The pan you cooked the pears in will have a lot of the caramelized sugar, butter, and pear juice left in it. First, measure the cognac (or other alcohol) into a small cup or bowl. For safety, it is important to add an alcoholic ingredient from a small container rather than from the original bottle. Set the pan over medium heat, and once the pan is hot, add the cognac, stirring to deglaze the pan. Then add the sugar. Once all is dissolved, stir the syrup over medium heat until deep brown. Take the pan off the heat and whisk in the butter and salt.

Remove the galette from the oven and let cool for 10 minutes.

While the galette is cooling, make the whipped cream: Whip the cream, confectioners' sugar, and almond extract in a chilled bowl until the cream holds soft peaks.

Cut the galette into wedges and serve with a dollop of whipped cream. Drizzle all with the pear caramel! So good!

CHESS PIE

EVIE · *This is my grandmother McGee's receipt and one of the ones that my mom and I discovered when we found my grandmother's long-lost receipt box. Chess pie is a classic Southern pie and this receipt is probably well over a hundred years old, but it certainly holds up.*

STEPHEN · *The origin of the name of this pie, like the name of many old dishes, is a matter of debate. There are a lot of theories, mostly regarding Southern mispronunciations: this is pie you store in your pie "chest"; it's not fancy, it's "just" pie; it originated in Chester, England; it was originally called "cheese pie." I don't believe any of them. Skip the debate and eat the pie.*

Makes 8 servings

1 unbaked 9-inch pie shell, homemade (recipe follows) or store-bought

1 cup packed light brown sugar

½ cup granulated sugar

¼ cup fine cornmeal

1 tablespoon all-purpose flour

2 large eggs

2 tablespoons sweetened condensed milk

1 teaspoon vanilla extract

8 tablespoons (1 stick) unsalted butter, melted

Heat the oven to 375°F with a rack in the lowest position. Stir the two sugars, cornmeal, and flour together in a large bowl just to break up any clumps of flour. (No one likes a lumpy chess pie.) It's helpful if the bowl has a handle.

Beat the eggs well in a small bowl, then beat in the condensed milk and vanilla. Pour the wet ingredients into the dry and beat with a whisk or handheld mixer until very smooth. Beat in the melted butter until you can't see even a trace of it.

Place the pie shell on a baking sheet, then pull out the lowest oven rack, set the baking sheet with the pie shell on the rack, and carefully pour the filling into the shell. Bake until the top of the pie is deep golden brown and the center is only a little bit jiggly, about 35 minutes. Cool for at least 2 hours before serving.

All-Purpose Food Processor PIE PASTRY

This recipe is courtesy of the extraordinarily patient man who tested and retested all our recipes, Chris Styler. Whether you need a shell for a sweet or for a savory filling, this recipe is easy to make and manages to be both flaky and sturdy at the same time. You can add a little more salt to the pastry if it is for a savory filling or, likewise, a little more sugar for a sweet filling.

**Makes enough for
2 single-crust 9-inch pies
or 1 double-crust 9-inch pie**

14 tablespoons (1¾ sticks) unsalted butter

2½ cups all-purpose flour

1 teaspoon salt

1 teaspoon sugar

8 to 10 tablespoons ice water

Cut the butter into small cubes. Put the butter in the freezer while you measure out the other ingredients.

Put the flour, salt, and sugar in the bowl of a food processor. Pulse a few times to mix. Scatter the butter over the flour and pulse quickly just until most of the mixture looks like very coarse cornmeal. The rest of the mixture will be coarser and there'll even be some pea-sized pieces. (This is the little secret most recipes don't tell you! It's OK—even necessary—for the butter to be of different sizes throughout.) Take the top off the processor bowl and sprinkle 8 tablespoons (½ cup) ice water over the soon-to-be-pastry. Pulse a few times and check the pastry by squeezing some between your fingers; the mixture should barely stick together. If it is at all crumbly, add some or all of the remaining water, 1 tablespoon at a time and blitzing as quickly as possible, until you get to that texture.

Turn the pastry out onto a lightly floured countertop. Push it together, kneading it very lightly, just to get the whole ball to stick together. Divide the dough in half and flatten each half into a rough circle. Smooth the edges of the circles with the side of your hand. (You'll be happy you made a nice round circle when it comes time to roll out the dough!) Wrap the pastry rounds in plastic wrap and refrigerate for at least 1 hour, and up to 2 days. Or, if you're making a one-crust pie, freeze one of the circles for later.

tip—To roll the pastry out to a nice even circle, roll from the edge closest to you all the way across and up to, but not over, the far edge—don't roll toward you. Between each pass with the rolling pin, give the dough a little turn. Flour the dough and countertop as needed.

Take the pastry out to come to room temp about 15 minutes before rolling it out. Flour the countertop lightly and flour the top of the dough. Roll out the pastry to a 13-inch circle (see Tip). Starting at one edge of the circle, roll the pastry up around the rolling pin, then unroll it over a 9-inch pie dish, centering it over the dish as best as you can. Gently press the pastry into the corners and up the sides of the pie dish. Trim the overhanging dough to ¾ inch and tuck that ¾ inch underneath to make a double-thick layer all around the edges of the pie plate. Crimp with your fingers or the tines of a fork. Refrigerate for at least 45 minutes, and up to 2 hours, before baking.

NOTE

• To blind-bake a pie shell: If your recipe calls for filling an unbaked shell, you're good to go once the shell is chilled. If you're looking for a blind-baked shell, do this: Heat the oven to 350°F with a rack in the center position. Line the pastry with parchment paper. Fill the lined shell about halfway full with pie weights, dried beans, or rice. Bake for 25 minutes. Remove the parchment with the weights and set aside so the weights can cool. Poke the bottom of the shell in several places with a fork. Bake until the bottom of the shell is a very light brown, about 10 minutes. The edges of the shell will be a little darker. Cool the shell completely before filling. The dried beans or rice can be stored and used again for this purpose.

Mrs. McGee's BOURBON CHOCOLATE PECAN PIE

EVIE • *There is a wonderful story behind this receipt. A few weeks after my mother died in November of 2022, one of my college roommates sent me a lovely note of condolence. In it she reminded me that not long after we graduated from college, she was working on a cookbook for her high school and my mother sent her this receipt to include in it. I had completely forgotten about this, and I know my mother had too. Mom and I spent months chatting about receipts, often while she was receiving treatment for her illness, but neither of us remembered this pie. Receiving the receipt again weeks after I lost Mom was such a gift to me. We baked the pie for our first Thanksgiving without Mom, and I felt her with me every step of the way. There is a lot of love in this delicious pie. I hope you will taste it too.*

STEPHEN • *I love that Evie received her mom's recipe from an old friend who remembered it and her so fondly. A taste of dishes our loved ones shared with us years before can instantly transport us back, gratefully, to tender and intimate moments. Long after those we love are gone, the gift of their food and the love that fed us lives on.*

Makes 8 servings

1 unbaked 9-inch pie shell, homemade (page 232) or store-bought

1 cup sugar

½ cup all-purpose flour

Large pinch of salt

2 large eggs

4 tablespoons (½ stick) unsalted butter, melted and cooled

2 tablespoons bourbon or more

1 cup pecans

1 cup chocolate chips

Whipped cream or ice cream for serving (optional)

Blind-bake the pie shell according to the package instructions or according to the Note on page 233. Let cool. Reduce the oven temp to 325°F.

Whisk the sugar, flour, and salt together in a large bowl. In a medium bowl, beat the eggs, melted butter, and bourbon together until smooth. Scrape the liquid ingredients into the dry and whisk briefly until the mixture is smooth. Stir in the pecans and chocolate chips.

Scrape the filling into the baked pie shell. Bake until the edges of the crust and the top of the pie are golden brown and the center is firm, about 50 minutes. Let cool completely.

If you like, serve the pie with whipped cream or ice cream.

FIG TARTS
for Ina

STEPHEN • *Every July we seem to have more figs, which leads me to think of more things to do with them, like this recipe for a simple Pop-Tart™–style mini fig tarts. I once made a batch and sent it to Ina Garten. She said she liked them, and I have no reason to doubt her honesty.*

EVIE • *I've never seen these before. You make them for Ina but not me?!*

Makes 10 to 12 tarts

½ recipe All-Purpose Food Processor Pie Pastry (page 232)

All-purpose flour for dusting

Fig Preserves (page 280) or the preserves of your choice, approximately a cup

2 tablespoons unsalted butter, melted

Sugar for sprinkling

Pat the pastry into a rough rectangle, wrap it well, and put it in the fridge for at least 1 hour, and up to a day.

Heat the oven to 425°F with a rack in the center position. Line a baking sheet with parchment paper. Dust the countertop lightly with flour.

Put the dough rectangle on the countertop and cut crosswise in half. Roll out one piece of dough into a rectangle about 15 inches long and 4 inches wide. Cut the pastry crosswise into 6 pieces (if you only get 5 pieces, no worries). Line up the pieces of pastry with one of the short ends facing you and plunk a rounded tablespoon of the preserves slightly off center of each one, with the preserves on the "you side" of the pastry. Fold the top of the pastry toward you over the filling so the ends and sides meet. Crimp all around with a fork, pressing firmly to seal. Line the crimped tarts up on the prepared baking sheet as you go. Repeat with the remaining pastry and preserves.

Brush the tops of the tarts with the melted butter and lightly sprinkle with sugar. Poke each tart once with a fork. Bake until golden brown, about 18 minutes, turning the pan around about halfway through baking.

Cool the tarts at least 30 minutes, but serve them, if you can, before they cool completely. Send some to Ina Garten.

HUGUENOT TORTE

STEPHEN • *I'm a Catholic, so I believe I need a special dispensation just to taste this. Bless me, Father, for I have snacked. Huguenot torte is an iconic Charleston dessert. Like any traditional dish, variations abound. This one features sliced apples and toasted almonds and has a little bit more topping than most versions.*

EVIE • *My mother told me that when she was newly married, she made this classic Charleston dessert for her in-laws and it totally collapsed into a runny mess. She was mortified and determined then and there to learn how to make it perfectly, which she did for many years. She would often serve it at one of the post-party 1:00 a.m. breakfasts she and my father hosted frequently when they were young. Stephen— why don't we ever do that?*

STEPHEN • *Because your parents were more fun than we are!*

Makes 12 servings

Softened unsalted butter for the baking dish

1 large Granny Smith apple, cored and cut into thin slices

¾ cup all-purpose flour

5 teaspoons baking powder

¾ teaspoon salt

4 large eggs, at room temperature

2 cups granulated sugar

2 cups toasted and chopped almonds

2 teaspoons almond extract

Confectioners' sugar for dusting

Ground cinnamon

Unsweetened whipped cream or almond whipped cream (page 229)

Heat the oven to 325°F with a rack in the center position. Grease an 8 × 12-inch (or similar size) baking dish with butter. Put the dish on a baking sheet. Scatter the apple slices in an even layer over the bottom of the dish.

Mix the flour, baking powder, and salt in a small bowl and set aside.

In the bowl of a stand mixer fitted with the paddle attachment, or in a medium bowl using a handheld mixer, beat the eggs on medium speed until very frothy. Gradually beat in the sugar and continue to beat until the eggs are fluffy and light yellow. Turn the mixer to low and add the toasted almonds and almond extract. Add the flour mixture and beat just until the flour is fully incorporated and no lumps remain—don't overmix.

Pour the batter over the apples and bake for about 45 minutes, or until the torte is crusty and brown on top. If serving the torte warm, let it stand for about 20 minutes before serving. Or cool to room temperature.

Either way, run a small knife along the sides of the pan before cutting into squares. Sift some confectioners' sugar over the top, dust with cinnamon, and add a dollop of whipped cream to each serving.

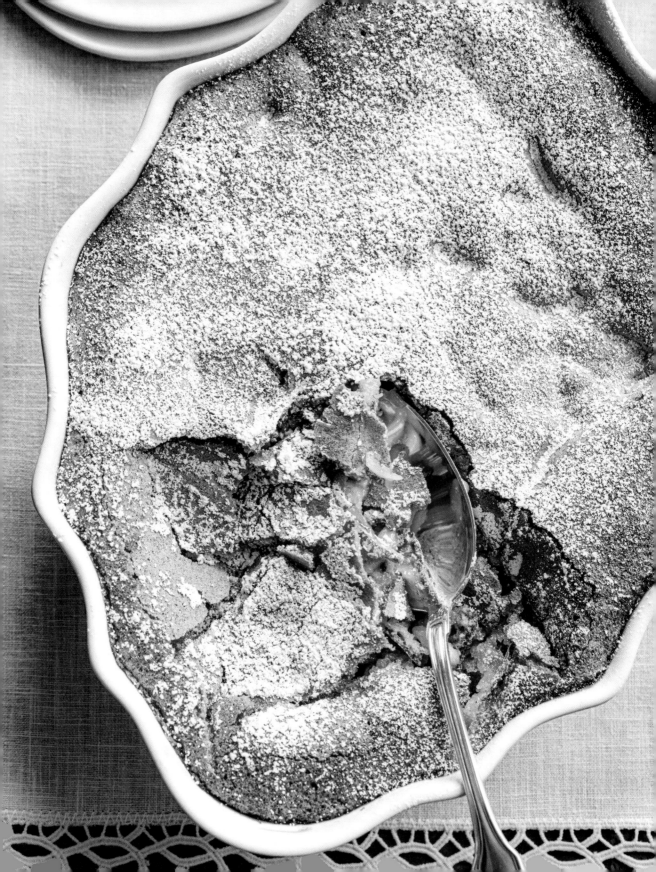

Another
CARROT CAKE

EVIE • *I love a good carrot cake, and this receipt is wonderful. It took me years to convince my kids to eat it though, because they thought I was trying to sneak a vegetable into their dessert, and they weren't having it. Maybe I should have called it something else. They never would have known it had carrots in it. We all love it now. Sometimes I make this for someone's birthday instead of the classic chocolate cake that the kids demanded when they were younger.*

STEPHEN • *Does the world need another carrot cake?*

EVIE • *Hell yes, the world needs another carrot cake! Just as much as the world needs another bourbon cocktail!*

STEPHEN • *That's getting kinda personal . . .*

Makes 12 servings

THE CAKE

1¾ cups canola oil, plus a little more for the cake pans

2 cups all-purpose flour, plus a little more for the cake pans

2 teaspoons baking powder

2 teaspoons baking soda

¾ teaspoon cinnamon

1 teaspoon salt

2 cups sugar

4 large eggs

3 cups grated carrots (about ¾ pound carrots)

¾ cup chopped walnuts

You'll need two 9-inch cake pans.

Heat the oven to 350°F with one rack in the upper third position and one in the lower third. Lightly oil and flour two 9-inch cake pans.

Make the cake: Sift the 2 cups flour, the baking powder, baking soda, cinnamon, and salt into a medium bowl. In the bowl of a stand mixer fitted with the paddle attachment, or in a large bowl using a handheld mixer, beat the sugar, the 1¾ cups oil, and the eggs together until a little lighter in color. Mix in the dry ingredients on low speed until just a few streaks of flour remain. Switch to a rubber spatula (remove the bowl from the mixer stand) and stir in the carrots and walnuts just until blended.

Divide the batter evenly between the prepared pans. Place one pan on each rack and bake until the cakes begin to pull away from the sides of the pans and a wooden pick poked into the center of the cakes comes out clean, about 25 minutes. If the cakes are coloring unevenly, rotate them gently after about 20 minutes of baking. Cool the cakes in the pans on cooling racks for about 20 minutes.

recipe and ingredients continued ⟶

Two 8-ounce packages cream cheese, at room temperature

8 tablespoons (1 stick) unsalted butter, at room temperature

1 pound confectioners' sugar (about 4 cups)

Flip the pans over onto the racks to remove the cake layers. Let cool completely.

Meanwhile, make the frosting: In the bowl of a stand mixer fitted with the paddle attachment, or in a large bowl using a handheld mixer, beat the cream cheese and butter until blended and very smooth. Sift the confectioners' sugar into the cream cheese mixture and beat on low speed until combined. Increase the speed to medium and beat until fluffy, about 2 minutes, stopping halfway through to scrape down the sides of the bowl.

Spoon enough of the frosting over the first layer of cake to make a nice—about 1 inch—layer. Stack the second layer of cake on top of that. Coat the top and sides of the cake generously with the remaining frosting.

Serve right away, or refrigerate the finished cake and then bring to room temperature for about 30 minutes before serving.

Stephen Candies Some
TANGERINE RIND

STEPHEN • *My mother made candied orange rinds at Christmastime. She would save up the peels in the freezer all year and then start boiling in December. Sometimes they were plain, sometimes half-dipped in dark chocolate. My help was limited to tasting. When she was tired or it was late, Mom wouldn't cut off the pith, then would kick herself, because the rinds would stay too wet, pick up too much sugar, and never properly dry out to crispy nibbles of sunshine. The first Christmas after Mom died, I started candying the peels. I use tangerine, so the pith isn't much of an issue (though I still say trim it off!). When the batches are done, I wrap them up and send them to my siblings in a cocktail kit to garnish with candied tangerine.*

EVIE • *Friends and family have often said to me when they open our freezer, "Why are there bags of orange rinds in here?" Now you know!*

Makes a lot

Lots of tangerine or orange peels

3 cups water

3 cups sugar

1 cup superfine or "castor" sugar, or as needed

Get out your tangerine rinds (which, of course, you have saved all year by popping them in the plastic bag you keep in your freezer for just this purpose). Boil them for a few minutes in a saucepan of water 3 times; drain the water and replace it with fresh water after each boil. Drain the peels and let cool.

Slice the peels into ¼-inch (or so) wide strips. It will be inexact, as the peels will be irregular. Then (and this is hard but important) use a small, sharp paring knife to slice off as much of the internal white pith of the peels as possible. The boiling will help soften and raise up the pith, but you will still be doing this for a while. Put on an audio book to keep you company, or a loooong podcast. I like Dan Carlin's *Hardcore History*. To remove the pith, place the strips, peel side down, on a cutting board. Press the knife side flat against the pith and, angling it down very slightly, slice away from you. The pith should cut/scrape right off.

Now that you have cleaned the peels of the bitter pith, bring the 3 cups water and granulated sugar combination up to a simmer (not a boil—the rinds are the candy, not the sugar mixture!). Add the prepared peels and simmer very gently for 45 minutes. Then cool in the syrup until the rinds can be handled but are still warm.

Have some orange syrup left?

• Use it to sweeten lemonade, iced tea, coffee, or tea.

• Substitute orange syrup for simple syrup in cocktails whenever a hint of orange might be welcome.

Using tongs, remove the peels one at a time and place on a cooling rack that has been very lightly oiled. Let the peels cool and dry until tacky, about 2 hours.

Place the superfine sugar in a bowl (with a handle, if possible) and add the peels one at a time, shaking the bowl to coat each peel and prevent clumping. Put the coated peels on wax paper and let dry. If there isn't enough sugar to coat the peels easily as you move through the coating process, add more sugar. (I usually leave them overnight.) If sealed tightly, they'll last indefinitely.

Sticky
TOFFEE PUDDING

EVIE • *This receipt was inspired by George Fowler, chef and co-owner of the Calypso Grill on Grand Cayman, whose sticky toffee pudding alone is worth the airfare. For Stephen's fiftieth birthday, I threw him a small dinner party. George's sticky toffee pudding is by far Stephen's favorite dessert, and I wanted to surprise him with it at the party. Serendipitously, George was in New York City the night of the party and offered to come in person and make it. To add a little fun, I announced to the room that I had flown George in from the Cayman Islands just to make the dessert. The idea that Evie McGee, a stingy Scots Presbyterian, would throw caution to the wind and do something that extravagant really added a little mystery to my reputation. I am at last coming clean here—it feels good to let you all know that I am in fact just as cheap as you all thought I was.*

STEPHEN • *I was one of the people convinced Evie had flown George up just to bake. That did not seem like my "breathtakingly levelheaded girl." But however she pulled it off, I was ecstatic. And drunk. When the plate was set in front of me with a very large slice fanned out in wedges, I inhaled it—then found out that it was six slices for the whole table to share. I would have been more embarrassed if I wasn't quietly slipping into a toffee coma.*

continued ⟶

Makes 9 servings

THE PUDDING

4 tablespoons (½ stick) unsalted butter, melted, plus more, unmelted, for the pan

1 cup pitted dates (Medjool preferred)

1 cup water

¾ cup packed dark brown sugar

2 large eggs, at room temperature

¼ cup molasses

2 tablespoons Lyle's Golden Syrup (see Note)

1¾ cups all-purpose flour

2 teaspoons baking soda

1¾ teaspoons baking powder

¾ teaspoon salt

THE SAUCE

1 cup heavy cream

½ cup packed dark brown sugar

¼ cup Lyle's Golden Syrup

½ teaspoon vanilla extract

Unsweetened whipped cream or vanilla ice cream for serving (optional)

> *tip*—Bring the water and dates up to a boil together; do not add the dates to boiling water.

Heat the oven to 350°F with a rack in the center position. Butter an 8-inch square baking pan and set it aside.

Make the pudding: Put the pitted dates and water in a small saucepan, bring to a boil over medium heat, and boil for 2 minutes. Set aside for a few minutes to cool, then put the dates and water into a food processor or blender and blend until smooth.

Whisk the brown sugar and the 4 tablespoons melted butter in a medium bowl until well combined. Add the eggs one at a time, whisking until smooth. Stir in the molasses, golden syrup, and date mixture just until blended. Do not overmix.

In a second bowl, combine the flour, baking soda, baking powder, and salt together. Add half of the dry mixture to the date mixture and stir until fully combined, then add the remaining dry mixture and stir until fully blended.

Scrape the batter into the prepared pan. Bake for 35 minutes, or until the pudding is firm around the edges and the center springs back when poked gently; a cake tester or wooden pick should come out clean.

Meanwhile, make the sauce: Put the cream and brown sugar in a small saucepan and stir together over low heat. Stirring continuously, slowly add the golden syrup and vanilla. Continue stirring over low heat until the sauce comes to a boil. Reduce the heat and simmer for 10 minutes. Remove the pan from the heat.

Remove the baked pudding to a cooling rack. Cool for about 15 minutes.

Poke several largish holes in the cake (the thick end of a chopstick works well) and pour about half the sauce over the top. The sauce will soak into the cake and make it even moister. Let cool for another 15 minutes or so, then cut into squares and drizzle a little of the remaining sauce over each serving. Top with whipped cream or ice cream, if you like.

NOTE

• Lyle's is a common British sweetener that can be found in some specialty and baking shops or online. If you can't find golden syrup, substitute an equal amount of light or dark corn syrup.

Cara's
ALMOND-BASIL COOKIES

STEPHEN • *There is a small but powerful cadre of bakers at* The Late Show *who occasionally surprise the rest of us with treats: waffle bars, baskets of muffins, cookie plates. This recipe is from writers' assistant Cara Washington, who is a very funny writer in her own right. She took a traditional Sicilian cookie, paste di mandorla, and added finely chopped basil, which adds a bright, fresh counterpoint to the rich fragrance of the almonds.*

EVIE • *We had totally forgotten about these delicious cookies until one morning when I was chatting with our wonderful UPS delivery guy, Duncan. I mentioned that Stephen and I were working on a cookbook together, and he said, "Don't leave out those incredible basil cookies." The previous Christmas we had given him a small batch as a holiday thank-you. Thanks to his reminder, here you are.*

Makes about twenty 2-inch cookies

Vegetable oil cooking spray, if needed

Confectioners' sugar

¾ cup granulated sugar

15 good-sized fresh basil leaves, torn into pieces

¼ teaspoon salt

2½ cups almond flour (aka almond meal)

2 large egg whites, at room temperature

Grated zest of 1 lemon plus 1 teaspoon juice

Heat the oven to 350°F with a rack in the center position. Line a baking sheet with parchment paper or spray lightly with cooking spray. Put a small scoop of confectioners' sugar in a shallow bowl.

Pulse the granulated sugar, basil, and salt in the bowl of a food processor just until the basil is coarsely chopped. Add the almond flour. Beat the egg whites with the lemon zest and juice in a small bowl, then add to the sugar mixture. Pulse just until the dough is blended—a few streaks of sugar or almond flour are OK. Scrape the dough out onto the countertop and knead gently a few times to finish mixing.

Roll rounded-teaspoon-sized pieces of dough into balls, dropping them into the confectioners' sugar as you go. When you have 4 or 5 dough balls, roll them around to coat them generously with sugar and move them to the prepared baking sheet, an inch apart. It's OK if some of the sugar falls off, but be sure the dough balls are well coated. Repeat with the remaining dough. Press down on the center of the cookies with your thumb to flatten them slightly and make a little indentation in the center of each.

Bake to the consistency you like: 15 minutes for a chewy cookie, or up to 20 minutes for a firmer crust and chewy center.

KEY LIME PIE

STEPHEN • *There is something electric and invigorating about the scent of a fresh Key lime. We are lucky to have two Key lime trees in the garden . . . which we have never used to make this pie. There are never enough ripe limes on the trees at one time, because someone (who shall remain me) keeps using them for cocktails.*

EVIE • *Key lime pie is my father's favorite dessert. When I was younger, there was hardly a Saturday in July that we didn't have a Key lime pie on the kitchen counter. It still tastes like summer to me.*

Makes 8 servings

THE CRUST

1½ cups graham cracker crumbs

8 tablespoons (1 stick) butter, melted and cooled

¼ cup sugar

THE FILLING

One 14-ounce can sweetened condensed milk

⅔ cup Key lime juice (see Note)

1 whole large egg plus 2 egg yolks

1 tablespoon grated Key lime zest (that you removed before juicing the limes)

1 teaspoon vanilla extract

¼ teaspoon salt

Unsweetened whipped cream for serving

Thinly sliced lime, for garnish

You'll need a shallow 9-inch pie plate.

Make the crust: With your fingertips, mush the graham cracker crumbs, melted butter, and sugar together in a medium bowl until the mix feels like wet sand. Firmly press the crumb mix into an even layer over the bottom and up the sides of a 9-inch pie plate. Refrigerate for at least 30 minutes, and up to several hours.

Heat the oven to 350°F with a rack in the center position. Put the pie plate on a baking sheet and bake until the crust is fragrant and lightly browned, 15 to 20 minutes. Cool the shell on the baking sheet while you're putting together the filling. Leave the oven on.

Whisk together the sweetened condensed milk, lime juice, egg, egg yolks, lime zest, vanilla, and salt in a medium bowl until thoroughly combined. Pour the custard mix carefully into the crust and bake until the edges of the filling are set but the center is still slightly jiggly, about 15 minutes. Remove from the oven and let cool to room temperature.

Pop the pie into the fridge for at least several hours before serving. Top each serving with a dollop of whipped cream and garnish with a lime slice.

NOTE

• If you can't find Key limes, substitute ½ cup regular lime juice plus 2½ tablespoons lemon juice.

THE COLBERT FUDGE
Sibling Saga

STEPHEN • *Colbert Fudge has been the center of much debate, mainly because it is one of the few recipes from my mom, and she never wrote it down. She just eyeballed it. For example, while we kids might say "3 to 6 tablespoons of butter," Mom would say "a piece of butter about the size of a medium egg." I didn't know eggs came in medium.*

I don't think it would hurt my mother's feelings to say that she was not a great cook. Eleven children did not leave much time to do much more than open a box of cereal and walk around the table, shaking it like a momma bird into our upturned mouths. But Mom could make this fudge, which is different from the soft bricks sold at tourist traps everywhere. (Why is fudge associated with vacation? Because after eating fudge, the idea of being productive seems impossible?) This fudge is somewhat grainy, not creamy, and the texture has more snap than traditional fudge. You'll know you have the texture right when the fudge breaks just a bit crisper than a peppermint patty. You'll know you have the sweetness right if, when you scrape it against your teeth, you think, "I should see a dentist."

EVIE • *This Colbert Fudge is a deeply held secret family receipt. So secret, in fact, that none of Stephen's siblings can agree on exactly how it is made. In an effort to be as democratic as possible, and to preserve family harmony, we solicited advice from Stephen's brothers and sisters. As per usual with the Colbert clan, each sibling had the correct answer, which they gave in their own particular style (see Ed's use of decimals!), and all the others were wrong! We tried lots of versions and the winner is listed last here. (A blend of Mary's and Ed's, I think.) This fudge is delicious, a power punch of sugary sweetness. Good luck, and whatever you do . . . don't let Jim, Ed, Mary, Margo, Tom, Jay, Lulu, or Stephen know which one you prefer.*

continued →

Margo's
DEFINITIVE RECIPE
FOR COLBERT FUDGE

MARGO • *"There's always time for fudge . . ."*

4 squares unsweetened chocolate

¾ cup sugar

¾ cup packed brown sugar

½ cup milk

6 tablespoons unsalted butter

1 teaspoon vanilla extract

Combine the chocolate, sugar, brown sugar, and milk in a saucepan. Melt the chocolate and stir often until the mixture forms a SOFT BALL in cold water (see my tip!). Remove from the heat and stir in the butter and vanilla. Stir briskly until glossy. Pour into a buttered dish. Enjoy.

Margo's tips: Don't forget about the "soft ball" test in cold water! For fudge sauce: Cook less and do not add the butter and vanilla.

Ed's
DEFINITIVE RECIPE
FOR COLBERT FUDGE

1.5 cups granulated sugar (extra-fine if you can get it, but Domino's will do)

.75 cup packed light brown sugar

.5 cup milk (can use any level of fat, whole, 2%, 1%, or skim; it affects cooking time and richness, so I recommend 2%)

4 squares Baker's unsweetened chocolate

3 to 4 tablespoons unsalted butter (or margarine)

1 teaspoon vanilla extract

Add the sugars and milk to a saucepan and melt together over low but direct heat. Add the chocolate and bring to a low boil. Stir regularly to avoid sticking and burning. Use a wooden spoon.

Continue to cook until the fudge creates a HARD BALL when dropped into cool water. If the ball is too soft, you have a terrific hot fudge sauce which will turn to a hard shell if poured over cold ice cream. For fudge, it needs to be a hard ball, but that just means it creates a defined drop and not a "spread out" drop.

Remove from the heat and stir in the butter and vanilla. I recommend cutting the butter into two or more chunks to speed the melting process. Whisk or stir vigorously while the butter is melting, and the vanilla will boil off its alcohol very quickly. Pour immediately into a buttered baking dish (ceramic or glass preferred). Do not forget to let one child lick the wooden spoon and the other scrape out the pan while the fudge is still warm. Let stand until hard, then cut and enjoy.

Will last for several days if stored tightly covered. Will dry out and harden if left out.

Mary's
DEFINITIVE RECIPE FOR COLBERT FUDGE

1½ cups granulated sugar

½ cup milk

4 squares unsweetened chocolate

4 tablespoons (½ stick) unsalted butter, plus more for the pan

1 teaspoon vanilla extract

Bring the sugar, milk, and chocolate to a boil, stirring.

Cook the syrup until it reaches the SOFT BALL stage (not hard ball). Test the syrup in cool, not cold, water.

Remove from the heat and beat in the butter and vanilla until the syrup is glossy. Pour into a buttered 8 × 8 pan.

The finished fudge should have a grainy texture.

Stephen's
DEFINITIVE RECIPE FOR COLBERT FUDGE

4 tablespoons (½ stick) salted butter, plus more for the pan

1 cup granulated sugar

½ cup packed brown sugar

½ cup milk

4 squares Baker's unsweetened chocolate

Vanilla extract

Butter an 8-inch square cake pan.

Stir the sugars, milk, and chocolate together in a medium saucepan. Bring to a boil, stirring constantly, and then stop stirring. Boil until about halfway between the soft ball and hard ball stage—what I call the "firm ball" stage. You're not looking for a hard, brittle ball, but more like the texture of that blue stuff that you use to stick things to the wall. Test often. If the mix dissolves when you drop it in the water, you have a way to go. If it forms a string, you're close. Keep a close eye on it from there.

Immediately remove from the heat and add the 4 tablespoons butter and a capful of vanilla; beat until shiny. Pour into the prepared pan.

Let the fudge set someplace cool for a few hours before cutting into squares. Or break it into pieces. Store the fudge in an airtight container at room temperature for days.

continued →

THE DEFINITIVE, DEFINITIVE RECIPE FOR COLBERT FUDGE (THE ONE THAT COUNTS)

Makes twenty-four 1½ × 2-inch pieces

4 tablespoons (½ stick) unsalted butter, plus more for the pan

1½ cups granulated sugar

½ cup whole milk

4 squares (2 ounces) Baker's unsweetened chocolate

1 teaspoon vanilla extract

Set a glass of cool water and the 4 tablespoons butter next to the stove. (See the sidebar.) Butter an 8-inch square cake pan and set it aside.

Stir the sugar, milk, and chocolate together in a medium saucepan over medium heat and bring to a boil, stirring occasionally. Once the syrup is boiling, stop stirring. Boil until about halfway between the soft ball and hard ball stage, aka "firm ball" stage. (Non-Colberts may use a candy thermometer and cook the syrup to 246°F.)

Immediately remove the pan from the heat and add the butter and vanilla; beat vigorously until the fudge is shiny and thickened a little. Pour into the prepared pan.

Let the fudge set someplace cool for a few hours before cutting into squares. Store in an airtight container at room temperature for days.

Last Words on the Colbert Fudge Saga:

MARGO TO ED AND STEPHEN: *"I have never had fudge last DAYS 🩶"*

TESTING SYRUP FOR FUDGE

Before you start boiling the syrup for fudge, set a glass of cool water and a spoon near the stove. To test the syrup, dip the spoon in the syrup and let the syrup drip into the water. At the soft ball stage (around 238°F), the little balls of syrup will hold together and you can make, well, a soft ball with them. The syrup has reached the hard ball stage (around 255°F) when you can easily remove the drops from the water and there is almost no give when you squeeze the ball. Firm ball is somewhere in between (around 246°F).

Fudgy BROWNIES

EVIE • *One of my favorite things to do with our kids when they were younger was to bake cookies or brownies together. Brownies were always fun, because the gooey batter got everywhere. These brownies are especially rich and yummy. They were inspired by one of the brownie recipes from* Charleston Receipts, *but with extra chocolate chips thrown in and a teaspoon of espresso powder for an added kick. If you are cooking with little children, warning: you might end up with a chocolate mess, but the deliciousness will be worth it.*

STEPHEN • *This may be the dessert chapter, but to me brownies are more accurately described as an over-the-counter antidepressant. You just can't stay sad or anxious while a warm brownie is in your mouth— which, if you watch the news too much, will be constantly.*

continued ⟶

Makes sixteen 2 × 2-inch brownies

6 tablespoons (¾ stick) unsalted butter, melted and cooled, plus more, unmelted, for the pan

⅔ cup all-purpose flour, plus more for the pan

¾ cup sweetened cocoa powder, preferably Ghirardelli

¼ teaspoon baking powder

¾ cup sugar

2 large eggs

1 teaspoon vanilla extract

1 teaspoon instant espresso powder (optional)

½ teaspoon salt

½ cup semisweet chocolate chips

Flaky salt, such as Maldon, for sprinkling (optional)

Heat the oven to 325°F with a rack in the center position. Lightly butter and flour an 8-inch square cake pan. Sift the cocoa powder, ⅔ cup flour, and baking powder together. Set aside.

In a medium bowl, vigorously whisk together the sugar, eggs, vanilla, espresso powder, if using, and salt until smooth and a little bit lighter in color. Beat in the melted butter until the mixture is smooth. Using a rubber spatula, fold in the dry ingredients just until combined and no flour clumps remain. Scrape down the sides of the bowl as you fold. Stir in about half of the chocolate chips.

Scrape the batter into the prepared pan and spread it out evenly. Scatter the remaining chocolate chips over the top. Sprinkle a small amount of flaky salt, if using, over the batter. Bake until the edges of the brownies are firm and the middle is still soft but set, 30 to 40 minutes. A cake tester or wooden pick should come out clean when you test the edges, but a little wet when you test the center. Cool completely before cutting.

LUCY'S ESPRESSO
COFFEE CAKE

264

BLUEBERRY MUFFINS

269

PAULA'S BANANA BREAD

272

GRANOLA

275

DROP BISCUITS

279

FIG PRESERVES

280

POPOVERS

283

MOM'S SHRIMP
AND HOMINY

286

HOMINY SURPRISE

291

BREAKFAST

This chapter comes near the end of the book because if your guests have a really good time at your dinner party, there's a chance they're staying for breakfast.

Most mornings we find ourselves pouring coffee down our throats just so we can get out the door on time, but on weekends and holidays, we like to serve up a big breakfast. Sure, part of the reason is that we hope the smell of bacon will waft upstairs and into the subconscious of our sleeping children and convince them to get out of bed and join the day, but we also like the fun of gathering around the kitchen table with pancakes or eggs and a full platter of bacon or sausage. Most of the recipes in this chapter are baked goods that we like to serve alongside the platters of eggs and bacon, but they are also yummy on their own with a hot cup of coffee. And although this chapter isn't very long, there are other candidates for breakfast throughout the book, because Stephen likes nothing better than to start the day with how he ended the one before. Whether it is a crab cake or red rice or a bowl of pulled pork, Colbert says throw a fried egg on that bad boy, and you're starting the day right!
• **EVIE**

Lucy's Espresso
COFFEE CAKE

EVIE • *Our niece Lucy Wichmann is an amazing cook. She is also a wiz with a spreadsheet and much more organized than either Stephen or I. Thank goodness Lucy agreed to help us gather and edit many of the receipts in this book, but this one is hers alone. It is delicious, really easy to make, and a winner for any brunch party. Thank-you to Lucy for allowing us to share it with you.*

STEPHEN • *I love coffee. I love cake. What could be better than a coffee cake made with coffee? I think you could also call this a "crumb cake," though I'm not sure what the difference is. As a child, I thought "crumb cake" referred to how messy it was to eat.*

Makes about 18 to 20 servings

THE CRUMBLE

8 tablespoons (1 stick) unsalted butter, melted and cooled to almost room temperature, plus more, unmelted, for the pan

1 cup all-purpose flour

½ cup packed light brown sugar

2 teaspoons cinnamon

Pinch of salt

Heat the oven to 350°F with a rack in the center position. Lightly butter a 13 × 9-inch baking pan.

Make the crumble: Stir together the flour, light brown sugar, melted butter, cinnamon, and salt in a medium bowl until all the ingredients are well blended and the mix is lumpy. Set aside.

> A stand mixer or powerful handheld mixer is key here. Check to be sure you have a 13 × 9-inch cake pan too.

recipe and ingredients continued ⟶

THE CAKE

⅔ cup sour cream

2 shots of strong espresso, or ¼ cup hot water plus 1 tablespoon instant espresso powder, stirred until dissolved

2 teaspoons vanilla extract

3½ cups all-purpose flour

2½ teaspoons baking powder

1½ teaspoons salt

½ teaspoon baking soda

1½ cups packed dark brown sugar

½ cup granulated sugar

12 tablespoons (1½ sticks) unsalted butter, at room temperature

½ cup vegetable oil

4 large eggs, at room temperature

Make the cake: Stir the sour cream, espresso, and vanilla together in a medium bowl until blended. Into another medium bowl, sift the flour, baking powder, salt, and baking soda together.

In the bowl of a stand mixer fitted with the paddle attachment, or in a large bowl using a handheld mixer, beat together the dark brown sugar, granulated sugar, butter, and vegetable oil until lightened up in color quite a bit, 4 to 5 minutes. Stop a few times to scrape down the bowl and paddle (or beaters). Add the eggs one by one, waiting for each to be incorporated before adding another; stop halfway through to scrape down the bowl and paddle. With the mixer on low, add the sour cream mixture and beat until well incorporated. Turn the mixer off and add the flour mixture. Mix on low speed until just a few streaks of flour are left. Finish mixing the batter with a rubber spatula, to avoid overmixing, and then clean the sides of the bowl and paddle one last time.

Pour the batter into the prepared pan and spread it out into an even layer. (An offset spatula works nicely for this.) Scatter the crumble evenly over the top of the batter, breaking up any really large lumps. Bake until a cake tester or wooden pick comes out clean, 40 to 45 minutes. Cool on a rack for at least 45 minutes before serving.

Wrap any leftover cake well (or store it in an airtight container). The cake will stay fresh for at least 2 days.

BLUEBERRY MUFFINS

EVIE • *Is there anything better than a warm, freshly baked muffin right out of the oven with a piping-hot cup of coffee? For years, Stephen and the kids would bring me breakfast in bed for Mother's Day, and it always included freshly baked muffins or scones. The kids would all pile on the bed with me and usually there were at least three muffins on the tray, which they gobbled up immediately. Thankfully they didn't drink coffee back in those days—so that was all mine! Try these delicious muffins on a day when you want to feel loved or share love with someone else.*

STEPHEN • *All the kids, to various degrees, depending on their various ages, got excited about Mother's Day breakfast. There was so much to do! Mix the batter, add the berries, grease the tins, scatter the flour, pet the dog. The eldest would carry the coffee. The middle child would carry the tray. And the youngest carried the newspaper. Things got a bit messy, and since everybody wanted to help, it took a little longer than the construction of the Panama Canal, so Evie had to patiently pretend to still be asleep by the time we got up there.*

Makes 12 muffins

Vegetable oil cooking spray

1¼ cups blueberries

2 cups all-purpose flour

½ cup sugar, plus more for topping the muffins

2½ teaspoons baking powder

½ teaspoon salt

¼ teaspoon cinnamon

1 cup whole milk

2 large eggs, well beaten

5 tablespoons unsalted butter, melted

Grated zest of 1 lemon or orange, or both

Heat the oven to 400°F with a rack in the center position. Use the cooking spray to grease a 12-muffin tin or line with muffin papers and spray the papers lightly. Toss the berries with 2 tablespoons of the flour and set aside.

Whisk the remaining flour, the ½ cup sugar, baking powder, salt, and cinnamon together in a medium bowl. In a small bowl, whisk the milk, eggs, and melted butter together thoroughly. Pour the wet ingredients into the dry, add the zest, and fold together a few times until the batter looks half-mixed. Gently fold in the blueberries, stirring as little as possible. It's OK if the batter is a little lumpy and you can see some small streaks of flour.

Spoon the batter into the prepared tin, dividing it evenly. The cups will be about three-quarters full. Sprinkle sugar generously over the tops.

Bake until the muffins are risen in the center and golden brown and a cake tester or wooden pick inserted in the center of a muffin comes out clean, about 20 minutes. Cool for at least 5 minutes before removing from the tin, and serve warm.

FUN WITH MUFFINS!

- Beat equal parts of room-temp butter and your favorite preserves/jelly/jam together until blended. Or beat softened butter with about half the amount of maple syrup or agave nectar. Serve a crock of any of the above with the warm muffins.

- If not all the muffins get scarfed down on Day 1, revive day-old muffins with a simple griddling: Heat a griddle or cast-iron or heavy nonstick pan over medium-low heat. Cut the muffins in half—across the equator or top to bottom, culinary minds differ on this one—and spread with a generous amount of softened butter. Grill butter side down until golden brown.

Paula's
BANANA BREAD

EVIE • *The world-renowned flutist Paula Robison has been a family friend of ours for years. She even played at our wedding. In my single days in NYC, I worked for Paula and her husband, violist Scott Nickrenz. Years ago, she shared with me her delicious receipt for banana bread, which I scribbled down on a notepad. I know the receipt by heart, but I still pull out the piece of paper, which is now over thirty-five years old, because it makes me smile to think of Paula and those happy days that I shared with her, Scott, and their daughter, Elizabeth. Our children grew up on this banana bread. In fact, John, our youngest, recorded a video for a fourth-grade project on how to "make something" using this receipt. Because the bread is so moist, the trickiest part of making it is figuring out when it is done. To keep the top from being too soupy or the ends from drying out, you start this bread at a higher temperature and turn it down to finish. Enjoy.*

STEPHEN • *I am grateful to the beautiful Paula Robison for many things she has given our lives—music and friendship and the example of her life as a great artist—but this banana bread is still high on the list. I think this might be the first food that Evie ever made me. No smell feels more like home.*

continued ⟶

Makes one 9 × 5-inch loaf; 12 servings

½ cup vegetable oil, plus more (or cooking spray) for the pan

3 ripe bananas, plus (optional) 1 banana for the topping

2 cups whole wheat flour, sifted

1 teaspoon baking soda

1 teaspoon cinnamon

½ teaspoon mace or nutmeg

½ teaspoon ground coriander

¼ teaspoon salt

⅓ cup wheat germ (optional)

½ cup sugar

½ cup honey

2 large eggs

½ cup raisins or chopped walnuts

Heat the oven to 350°F with a rack in the center position. Grease a 9 × 5-inch loaf pan with vegetable oil or cooking spray. Mash the ripe bananas well in a medium bowl.

Sift together the whole wheat flour, baking soda, cinnamon, mace, coriander, and salt into a medium bowl, then stir in the wheat germ, if using, until mixed.

In the bowl of a stand mixer fitted with the paddle attachment, or in a large bowl using a handheld mixer, beat the ½ cup vegetable oil, sugar, honey, and eggs together on medium-low speed until well combined and lighter in color, about 3 minutes. Scrape down the bowl, add the mashed bananas, and mix on low speed until blended into the egg mix. Scrape down the bowl and paddle/beaters and add the dry ingredients. Beat at low speed just until no streaks of flour remain; don't overbeat. Remove the bowl from the mixer stand, if necessary, and fold in the raisins with a rubber spatula, scraping down the bowl as you go.

Scrape the batter into the prepared pan. If you're using the whole banana for topping, slice it lengthwise and arrange the halves on the top. Bake for 20 minutes. Lower the oven temp to 275°F and bake until a cake tester or long wooden pick poked into the center of the bread comes out clean, about 1 hour and 15 minutes.

Cool the bread on a rack for about half an hour, then invert the bread onto the rack, set right side up, and cool completely (if you can hold out that long) before slicing. The banana bread will keep well tightly wrapped or in an airtight container for up to 3 days.

GRANOLA

EVIE • *I have tried lots of receipts for granola over the years, but the best by far is this one that my friend Anne Dickerson shared with me. The fun thing about it is you can add or substitute as you want. If I can't find pumpkin seeds, then I substitute with sunflower seeds, or if I don't have dried cranberries on hand, I use raisins. I love this so much that one Christmas I gave out batches to friends as my holiday gift.*

STEPHEN • *We eat this by the handful. It also makes the house smell amazing. Every time Evie makes it, I think, "We should sell the house today. One whiff of this place, and they'd be submitting sealed bids." Ev is right, you can substitute many of the ingredients, or all of them and just drink gin, which is mostly what we do with the Dickersons. The recipe: 1) Chill gin. 2) Drink. 3) Laugh with friends.*

✳
pictured on page 277

Makes about 3 clumpy quarts

4 cups old-fashioned (not instant) oats

1 cup raw cashews

1 cup dried cranberries

¾ cup sunflower or pumpkin seeds

½ cup sliced almonds

½ cup coconut oil

½ cup honey

½ cup maple syrup

1 teaspoon vanilla extract

½ teaspoon cinnamon

½ teaspoon salt

Heat the oven to 350°F with one rack in the upper third position and one in the lower third. Line two large rimmed baking sheets with parchment paper.

Toss the oats, cashews, cranberries, sunflower seeds, and almonds together in a large bowl. Do this using your hands to really mix things up. In a small bowl, whisk together the coconut oil, honey, maple syrup, vanilla, cinnamon, and salt until the mixture is thickened, smooth, and a lovely caramel color. Pour the wet ingredients over the dry ingredients and mix until the dry ingredients are coated. Use your hands again to really get the syrupy mixture to coat the dry ingredients thoroughly.

Spread the granola out onto the prepared baking sheets, dividing it evenly. Bake until the granola is deep honey-brown, 20 to 30 minutes, stirring and turning the granola once about halfway through. Keep an eye out—once the granola starts to brown, it will take on color quickly.

Cool the granola completely on the baking sheets, then break into clumps and store in an airtight container.

DROP BISCUITS

EVIE • *As we were doing research for this cookbook, my mother suggested that I should look for my grandmother's receipt box. My paternal grandmother, Madeleine Stoney McGee, was an excellent cook, but she died when I was very young and the only thing I remember about her cooking was that she would serve me and my sister white bread with butter and sugar on top. (I loved it!) One afternoon I was with my mother going through her attic storage space and we stumbled upon Grandmother's receipt box. It was like finding a buried chest. We both squealed with delight. These drop biscuits were one of the treasures we discovered. They are delicious and a Southern classic, grandma-style.*

STEPHEN • *These are very much like the scones the kids and I would sometimes make for Mother's Day, if we forgot to get blueberries (see Blueberry Muffins, page 269). These simple, quick breads are easy to make, and they're easy to make savory by adding shredded cheese and herbs to the dough. By the way, I also had white bread and sugar sandwiches as a boy, but my binding agent was not butter—it was mayonnaise. For some reason, Evie thinks that is disgusting, and for many reasons, she is right.*

Makes about 12 biscuits

Vegetable oil cooking spray or vegetable oil (if needed)

2 cups self-rising flour

¼ teaspoon salt

8 tablespoons (1 stick) cold unsalted butter, cubed

½ cup very cold whole milk

Room-temp salted butter for serving

Fig Preserves (page 280) or other fruit preserves for serving (optional)

Heat the oven to 425°F with a rack in the center position. Grease a baking sheet with cooking spray or vegetable oil, or line it with parchment paper.

In a medium bowl, whisk the flour and salt together. Add the butter and rub it with your fingertips until all of the butter looks like shaggy cornflakes. Pour in the milk and stir with a fork to make a dough that just holds together. Don't overmix.

Drop by heaping tablespoonfuls onto the prepared baking sheet. The dough blobs should be about 1½ inches across. Bake until golden brown in spots and a biscuit feels light when you pick it up, 18 to 20 minutes. Serve warm with butter and, if you have it, fig or other preserves.

FIG PRESERVES

EVIE • *We have several fig trees at our house in South Carolina. Every summer, as the fruit begins to ripen, there is a mad dash to pick all the figs before the birds descend. We made up this receipt one year when we had more figs than we could eat. These preserves are equally delicious on a piece of buttered toast or over a scoop of vanilla ice cream. They can also be used to fill the Fig Tarts for Ina (page 237) or as a topping for baked Brie (see the sidebar).*

STEPHEN • *On our lot, we grow some citrus, along with Turkish and Celeste fig trees. Though I think the Turkish are better eating and prettier, both make a great jam. Round about 4th of July every year, they start to come ripe, and once they do, it's bucketsful every day. As it's high summer, I like to stay cool by climbing behind the outer canopy of the tree and picking from the inside out, while the sun shines through the huge fuzzy leaves—which any medieval painting will tell you make a quick and stylish bikini bottom.*

Makes about 6 cups

2 quarts ripe figs
(about 4 pounds)

½ cup water

1 cup sugar

Small pinch of salt

Grated zest and juice
of 1 lemon or 1 tablespoon
balsamic vinegar

½ vanilla bean, split
lengthwise

Rinse the figs lightly under cold water and drain them well. Cut off the stem tips and quarter the figs. Combine the figs and water in a large, heavy pot and bring to a boil over medium heat. Reduce the heat to a slow boil. Cover the pot and cook, stirring occasionally, until the figs are jammy, 15 to 20 minutes.

Stir in the sugar and salt and turn the heat to low. Cook, uncovered, stirring frequently to avoid scorching, until the preserves are very thick, about 15 minutes. Add the lemon juice and zest and the split vanilla bean. Cover and cook for an additional 5 minutes.

Spoon the hot preserves into clean glass canning jars, seal the lids tightly, and store at room temperature.

BAKING BRIE

Choose a small (around 14-ounce) Brie (or Camembert). Heat the oven to 350°F with a rack in the center position. Put the Brie on a parchment-lined small baking sheet or into a baking dish that holds the cheese snugly. Bake until the Brie feels very soft in the center when poked, about 20 minutes. Move the cheese to a cutting board or serving platter (not necessary if you used a baking dish). Drizzle a small amount of honey over the top, if you like. If you have some thyme or rosemary sprigs, scatter them over the cheese as well. Serve with sturdy crackers or crostini and a bowl of the fig preserves. Or warm the preserves and spoon them over the hot Brie.

POPOVERS

EVIE · *We have spent many happy vacations in Maine as a family. In fact, my sister took our son Peter on a camping trip to Maine when he was just nine years old. It was on this trip that Peter discovered popovers. He was very impressed with the "popping over" aspect and immediately learned how to make them from scratch, just so he could see them rise and spill over the muffin tins. His little brother, John, soon joined in. We all love these light and airy popovers. Just one bite, and we are back on the trails of Acadia National Park!*

STEPHEN · *My first memories of these are not as popovers, but as their British cousin, Yorkshire pudding. When I was twelve, after a long day of tramping around London looking at Beefeaters and gothic arches with my mother and sister Lulu, we sat for dinner at a venerable old restaurant, Simpson's in the Strand. We were exhausted and taciturn, and the restaurant staff took such pleasant care of us. I remember being lent a child's-sized tie by the coatroom clerk, as such were required. I remember great beefs on rolling, domed trolleys. But mostly, I remember the Yorkshire pudding—not really pudding at all, I thought, but warm and comforting, and hollow. I could have crawled inside and nodded off.*

Popovers are puffy, warm, and crisp on the outside, and moist inside. They are a good for any meal, because pretty much anything is good on them—butter, jam, honey, maple syrup, gravy, pan juices from roast chicken or beef . . . go nuts.

Makes 12 large popovers

A popover pan is nice to have, but a muffin tin will do.

3 tablespoons unsalted butter, plus more for greasing the cups and surface of the muffin tin

4 tablespoons (½ stick) unsalted butter, melted, for the bottoms of the muffin tin

1 cup all-purpose flour

½ teaspoon salt

1 cup whole milk

3 large eggs, at room temperature

Heat the oven to 450°F with a rack in the lowest position. (Make sure there isn't another rack directly above, as popovers rise quite a bit.) Even after you hear the ding that tells you the oven is preheated, let it heat for another 10 minutes. Oven temp is key here!

Grease each muffin cup in a 12-cup muffin tin and the top surface of the tin using unmelted butter. Add 1 teaspoon melted

continued ⟶

butter to each cup. Place the tin in the preheating oven. You will be pouring the batter into the hot cups.

Sift the flour into a small bowl. Stir in the salt. Heat the milk and the 3 tablespoons butter together in a small saucepan over the lowest heat possible. When the butter is melted, pour the milk mixture into a medium bowl, add the eggs, and beat until a little foamy. Whisk in the flour until the batter is mostly smooth—a few small lumps here and there won't hurt.

Carefully remove the hot tin from the oven and pour about 3 tablespoons of batter into each muffin cup—they should be about half full. Bake until the popovers are "popped" and deep golden brown, 20 to 25 minutes. Let stand in the tin for 5 minutes before serving.

tip—After popping the popovers into the oven, don't open the oven door for any reason until at least 20 minutes into the baking. Keep the oven light on to gauge doneness.

safety tip

Do not remove the hot popovers with bare hands.

Mom's SHRIMP and HOMINY

EVIE • *Charlestonians eat shrimp and hominy for breakfast. My father, who was born in 1929 and has lived in Charleston his entire life, says Charlestonians have always called grits "hominy," and he doesn't know why. Technically, hominy is whole kernels of corn that have been soaked in lye, which can cause some confusion because what we really mean is ground hominy grits! If you can find stone-ground grits, that is what we recommend. This is much better than instant grits, but either will work.*

Our children love shrimp and hominy for breakfast or anytime. We often make it for Sunday night dinner, as it is quick and easy. This is the simple and "pure" way to make it, but there are lots of options for spicing things up. You can add cheese and garlic to the hominy or even bacon. But whatever you do, make sure you spoon a little bit of the pan "liquor" over the shrimp and hominy once you plate it. You won't want any of that delicious sauce to go to waste.

STEPHEN • *Charlestonians have peculiar names for many things. For instance, the classic Charleston single houses don't have porches, they have "piazzas." Lima beans are "sivvys." And very early on in our relationship, I was informed that the McGees, as bastions of Charlestonian tradition, did not eat grits—they eat hominy. Why? I think it just sounds more refined to say when you're sitting on the piazza.*

continued —→

Makes 4 very generous or 6 "regular" servings

THE HOMINY

Salt

1 cup stone ground grits (see headnote)

4 tablespoons (½ stick) unsalted butter

THE SHRIMP

4 tablespoons (½ stick) unsalted butter

2 pounds large (26–30 count) shrimp, peeled (tails removed!) and deveined (see page 20)

1 tablespoon lemon pepper, homemade (page 100) or store-bought

2 tablespoons dry white wine

Grated zest and juice of 1 lemon

1 tablespoon chopped fresh dill, plus more for serving, or 1 teaspoon dried dill (optional)

Salt if needed

> *tip*—Lay out the prep for the shrimp before you start cooking the grits. Once the grits are done and being kept warm, cook the shrimp quickly and bring it all together.

Make the hominy: Bring 4 cups of water to a boil in a Dutch oven or other large pot over medium heat. Add about a teaspoon of salt. Slowly pour the hominy into the boiling water while vigorously whisking to avoid lumps. Switch to a wooden spoon and cook, stirring occasionally (but more toward the end), until the hominy is fully cooked and thick enough to mound a little on the spoon, about 20 minutes. Taste and add more salt if needed. Cover the pot, remove from the heat, and let sit until the shrimp are ready.

Make the shrimp: Melt the butter in a large skillet over medium heat. Add the shrimp and season with the lemon pepper. Cook the shrimp, turning once, until pink, opaque, and cooked through, about 2 minutes per side. Pour in the wine and let it bubble up for a minute, then stir in the lemon zest, lemon juice, and dill. Add salt if needed. Remove from the heat.

Plate it up: To serve this family-style, spoon the hominy into a large shallow bowl and ladle the shrimp and pan liquor over it. Or, to serve on individual plates, ladle the hominy and shrimp side by side on the plates and spoon the pan liquor over them. Scatter a little fresh dill over everything, if you like.

variations

VARIATION 1: Shrimp and Cheesy Hominy: When the grits are fully cooked, just before covering the pot, stir in 1 to 1½ cups grated sharp cheddar cheese.

VARIATION 2: Bacony Shrimp and Hominy: Cook a few strips of bacon in the pan you'll be using for the shrimp until nice and crisp. Move the cooked bacon to a small bowl. Pour off most but not all of the fat. Cook the shrimp in the pan as described above. Crumble up the cooked bacon, stir into the finished shrimp or hominy, and serve.

VARIATION 3 (IN CASE OF HANGOVER): Make the Cheesy Hominy and serve with the Bacony Shrimp.

HOMINY
Surprise

EVIE • *Hominy surprise is another classic Charleston receipt. For some reason, I am not sure why, it was reserved for special occasions in my house. We served hominy surprise only if we were having a brunch party or if my parents were hosting a post-party 1:00 a.m. breakfast, as they did every so often. Stephen and I don't have parties starting at 1:00 a.m. It is a bitter pill to swallow that your parents were more fun than you are.*

STEPHEN • *Surprise! It's more hominy. For most of the last 150 years, there was very little money in the Lowcountry, and cornmeal is so cheap it's almost free, so the old cookbooks are full of dishes like this that both filled a belly and pinched a penny. Because it takes on the flavor of anything you add, some have called hominy the tofu of the South. Not many, but some. So far just me, but it's gonna catch on.*

Makes 8 servings

1 tablespoon unsalted butter, plus more for the baking dish

1 tablespoon salt

2 cups stone ground grits

1 cup whole milk

2 large eggs

2 teaspoons to 1 tablespoon Worcestershire sauce

½ teaspoon freshly ground pepper

2 cups grated sharp cheddar cheese (about 6 ounces)

Heat the oven to 350°F with a rack in the center position. Butter an 8-cup (2-quart) baking dish—an 8 × 11-inch dish works well.

Bring 8 cups of water to a boil in a large Dutch oven or other heavy pot over medium heat. Stir in the salt and then slowly pour the hominy into the boiling water while vigorously whisking to avoid lumps. Switch to a wooden spoon and cook, stirring occasionally (but more toward the end), until the hominy is fully cooked, about 20 minutes; adjust the heat so the hominy doesn't stick or "erupt" in spots. Take the pot off the heat as soon as the hominy is done.

Whisk the milk, eggs, Worcestershire sauce, and pepper together in a medium bowl. Stir the 1 tablespoon butter into the hominy until it's melted, then add the egg mixture all at once and stir until blended. Stir in 1 cup of the cheese. Scrape the mixture into the buttered baking dish and top with the remaining 1 cup cheese.

Bake until the edges of the hominy are set but the center is still jiggly, about 1 hour. Let stand for at least 15 minutes before serving, and up to 25 minutes for a firmer texture.

ESPRESSO MARTINI

298

BASIL MARTINI

301

APEROL SPRITZ

302

OLD FASHIONED

305

BUZZ FUZZ

306

THE COLBERT BUMP

308

CAPRI SUNSET

311

LES PIEDS
DANS L'EAU

313

DRINKS

I love cocktail hour. It feels like a reward. For having gone so long without a cocktail. I love the warm and boundless greeting, "What can I get you?" I love the equipment of the well-appointed bar—the jigger, the strainer, the shaker, the ridiculously long spoon. And because you are, literally, using a "spirit" to make a potion that changes the mind and loosens the tongue, cocktails have an alchemical quality that appeals to a lover of fantasy fiction. I can picture Paracelsus happily whipping up a fresh batch of homunculi in a retort brimming with bourbon and bitters.

My earliest memory of making a cocktail is for Aunt Margaret. She was my father's twin and a very funny, if somewhat frightening, figure. If memory serves, her drink, like my dad's, was bourbon and branch (water)—simple enough for an eager young boy to fix. I would run to the kitchen, probably get help from a sibling, and then return with the full glass as carefully as a tightrope walker on a windy day.

I would hand it to Margaret, who would invariably look over her glasses and say, "You're a rotten kid."

Far too many years later, I called Margaret. When she picked up, I said, "Margaret, it's Jim's son."

She said, "Which one?"

"The rotten one," I answered.

"How rotten?"

"The rottenest," I said.

"How are you, Stephen?"

That story doesn't have much to do with drinks, other than this: I'd love to throw my arms around those twins and say, "What can I get you?" • **STEPHEN**

Espresso MARTINI

EVIE • *I don't remember when exactly it happened, but the first time Stephen tasted an espresso martini I think his entire worldview changed. Here was something that combined two of his favorite things in the world: caffeine and alcohol. No matter where we went on vacation, he would always kick off the holiday by ordering one. Then during Covid, when we were all isolated in our house doing* The Late Show *from our library, he decided to bring the vacation home. Every night after we taped the show, he would close the laptops and iPads and shut the door to the library/studio, walk ten feet to our bar, and make himself an espresso martini. Maybe it was the vodka or maybe it was the caffeine or maybe it was the mood enhancement, but he didn't catch Covid. Whatever it takes!*

STEPHEN • *I am grateful to Jon Stewart for many things, not the least of which is my Nespresso™ machine, which stood largely unused until Covid lockdown, when I realized I could make my own espresso martinis even though the bars were all closed. I toasted him constantly.*

Makes 1 cocktail

2 ounces vodka

1 ounce Kahlúa or other coffee liqueur

2 dashes Fee Brothers' Aztec Chocolate Bitters (see Note)

A shot of hot freshly made espresso

Whole espresso beans or a small dusting of very fine espresso grounds, for garnish (optional)

Combine the vodka, Kahlúa, and bitters in a cocktail shaker, then add the espresso. Immediately add a healthy cup of ice to the shaker. Cover and shake for at least 30 seconds. Pour into a chilled martini glass. The foam will form a nice frothy layer, on which you might float a few coffee beans or a dusting of very fine coffee grounds, if using.

Wash out the shaker. You're going to want a second one as soon as possible.

NOTE

• Fee Brothers is a family-owned maker of top-notch bitters in a wide variety of flavors—including Aztec Chocolate. If your local liquor store doesn't carry Fee Brothers bitters, they are available from multiple online sources.

Basil
MARTINI

STEPHEN • *I had this one night when I was out with my sister Lulu. It was so good that I tried to re-create it when I got home. It took many (very pleasant) attempts, but I think I eventually nailed it. The drink is the pretty pale green of early spring. Pace yourself—it's so refreshing you might be tempted to chug.*

EVIE • *This is such a fun drink to make. The mint and basil make the house smell like springtime, plus you get to say the word "muddle" and mean it!*

Makes 1 cocktail

6 fresh basil leaves
4 fresh mint leaves
1 ounce simple syrup
3 ounces vodka

tip—Mint is a generous perennial. Plant it once, and you'll never go mintless again.

Put the basil and mint in a cocktail shaker. Add the simple syrup and muddle the leaves together. Pour in the vodka, add enough ice to fill the shaker about two-thirds full, cover, and shake for at least 30 seconds. Strain into a chilled martini glass.

Stephen says

Because this has so many bits of leaves floating in it, it may clog the cap holes when you pour it, so I recommend you use a Hawthorne strainer. I didn't know the name either—I looked it up. You may know it as the bar tool that looks like a paddle with a tiny slinky wrapped around one end. Use that to cover the mouth of the shaker, and pour.

Aperol
SPRITZ

STEPHEN • *While Ev and I are latecomers to the Aperol parade, this refreshing drink has been the go-to for our friend Carrie Byalick for many years. I would have something simple and stiff, like bourbon and soda, and she would order what looked to me like it barely required legal age to order. I have come around in a big way. Not only does this delicious drink pour down the throat like transubstantiated Gatorade, it has the most beautiful Murano glass color. I like to serve it with one large ice cube so the sun can shine right through to place a puddle of red-orange light in your hand.*

EVIE • *We finally joined the Aperol Spritz party in the summer of 2022 when we took a family trip to Provence, France. Even though Aperol is technically from Italy, we designated it as the mascot and mission of our entire vacation. Daily consumption was required and happily achieved.*
    "Easy as 3–2–1."

Makes 1 drink

3 parts Prosecco
2 parts Aperol
1 part sparkling water
An orange slice, for garnish

Fill a large glass half full of ice. Pour in the Prosecco and then the Aperol and sparkling water. Give it a quick stir and garnish with the orange slice.

A variation with a touch more punch to settle those shaky hands

Add Stoli Orange or other orange vodka—a half-jigger for every serving.

OLD FASHIONED

STEPHEN • *This cocktail is called the Old Fashioned because it was a very early drink in American bars. As cocktails became more common, anyone wanting the original cocktail would say, "Give me that old-fashioned one."*

For something with such a long history and such a simple recipe, there are many disagreements over the proper preparation. Mine is by no means definitive, just correct, and is marked mostly by the use of uncommon sweet elements: cherry syrup and candied tangerine rind (page 244).

EVIE • *One of the many things I love about my husband is that he is part seventeen-year-old and part seventy-year-old—his love of making this drink belongs to the seventy-year-old, and I find his obsession charming. I also know it was his mother's favorite drink, and when he makes it, he thinks of her.*

Makes 1 cocktail

2 ounces rye whiskey or high-rye bourbon (such as Maker's Mark)

2 dashes Fee Brothers' Old Fashion Aromatic Bitters (or Angostura, if you insist)

1 strip candied tangerine rind (see page 244) or fresh rind, if that's what you've got

1 teaspoon Luxardo Maraschino cherry syrup (or less; I like my OF not too sweet)

1 Luxardo cherry (see Note)

Combine the whiskey and bitters in a rocks glass, then drop in the candied rind to soak for a minute and let the sweetness and citrus oils meld with the liquor. Add the cherry syrup and cherry. Stir until the syrup is thoroughly mixed in. Top with ice and mix again. The melting ice mellows the heat of the whiskey.

This cocktail takes a moment to get right and a connoisseur of the Old Fashioned will use this time to talk to the recipient and discuss the fine ingredients, or simply contemplate that the time each properly mixed drink requires is the only thing slowing you down.

Enjoy.

NOTE

• Luxardo cherries are key to making a memorable Old Fashioned. They are more like a candied cherry than those supersweet, bright-red maraschinos. Luxardos are packed in a thick, rich syrup, which is what makes them so special. If you can't find them in a brick-and-mortar, they are easy to find online.

BUZZ FUZZ

STEPHEN • *This is a great summer drink, not just because it will cool you down. Summer-ripened peaches are essential ingredients. We are lucky enough to have a friend, Butler Derrick, who most years gifts us a brimming basket of freestone peaches from his family farm right before the 4th of July. They are about the size of a Chicago softball and hard as a rock, but three days later, they start coming ripe at an alarming pace. The cobbler levels become dangerous, everyone's chin is dripping, and white shirts* are not advised.*

(*Side note: When Evie and I were dating, we spent the weekend with some good friends and some great peaches. I said something about being as careful as Prufrock about the juice because the stains never come out. Evie doubted peach juice was a forever stain. I immediately rubbed my half-eaten peach on my "HA! Comedy Network" shirt. I saved the shirt. It's still stained. I can't believe she continued to date me. I'm impossible.)

EVIE • *Not only do I now understand much much more about "The Lovesong of J. Alfred Prufrock" than I did when I was twenty-eight, I understand more about Stephen Colbert than I did then as well. Never challenge him about random information like fruit stains or any sort of obscure fact; he is (nearly) always right and will never let you forget it!*

STEPHEN • *I am not coming off great in this story . . .*

Makes 8 large cocktails, or 1 cry for help

12 ounces (1½ cups) golden rum (I like Mount Gay)

2 to 3 very ripe halved and pitted peaches, plus peach slices, for garnish

One 12-ounce container frozen limeade

4 cups ice cubes

Throw all of the ingredients (except the peach slices) into the cup of a blender. Blend until very smooth, then serve immediately, garnished with peach slices, and relax.

Don't wear a white shirt.

The Colbert
BUMP

STEPHEN • *Back in 2009, on what must have been a very slow week for* The Colbert Report, *we asked cocktail historian Dave Wondrich to join me to talk about cocktail culture and, while there, to make up a drink: "The Colbert Bump." "Bump" sounded a bit like "bounce" to him, and George Washington's favorite drink was a Cherry Bounce— brandy with mashed cherries, sugar, and spices. Inspired by the FoOC (Father of Our Country), Dave invented The Bump—with an extra dose of gin, just to kick in your wooden teeth.*

EVIE • *We often serve this drink at our parties. It is delicious and a crowd favorite. We make pitchers of it. But beware: it's a strong drink, and as the night goes on . . . things might start bouncing.*

Makes 1 cocktail

1 ounce Heering cherry liqueur
1½ ounces gin
¼ ounce lemon juice
Splash of soda water

Fill a tall iced tea glass
three-quarters full of ice.
Add the ingredients in
the order listed. Stir and
serve with a heavy dose of
pomposity.

CAPRI SUNSET

STEPHEN • *I am occasionally lucky enough to have drinks with Dick Cavett. Ol' Dickie always gets the same thing: Campari and orange juice. Marlon Brando introduced Dick to it, and the lesson took. No offense to Marlon, but I like my drinks lighter and stronger, so I add a healthy splash of soda water and an unhealthy shot of vodka. The final product looks like a cross between a Tequila Sunrise and a Capri Sun, so . . . Capri Sunset.*

EVIE • *Believe me, there were times when our kids were young that I was ready to pour a little vodka into a Capri Sun pouch myself. This is better!*

Makes 1 cocktail

2 ounces orange juice
1 ounce vodka
Soda water
1 ounce Campari

Fill a tall glass with ice. Pour in the orange juice, vodka, and enough soda water to almost fill the glass. Stir gently, then "float" the Campari on top of the drink and let it settle gently to the bottom.

Les Pieds
dans L'eau

STEPHEN • *The year we were in Provence with our large and thirsty family, a brutal heatwave was gripping southern Europe, so our expat gastronomical guide, Jane, whipped up a refreshing pitcher of wine and fruit that inspired this recipe. Jane originally used local muskmelon, which, in August in the South of France, is incredibly sweet. Here in the States, even the ripest cantaloupe (a type of muskmelon) I can find doesn't have the flavor to anchor this summertime cooler. So I switched to watermelon—just the taste of which is like turning on an air conditioner in my soul.*

EVIE • *I think that watermelon is a great ingredient here, because the phrase "les pieds dans l'eau" means "feet in the water," a French expression roughly equivalent to "let your hair down." During our trip to Provence, we adopted this as our family motto. Our hope for you, as you finish this book, is that you let your hair down, put your feet in the water, and enjoy good food, good drinks, and good times with those you love.*

Makes 6 or so tall drinks

2 cups watermelon juice
Fresh mint sprigs
2 cups muscat wine

Watermelon juice is easy: Drop the red flesh (no seeds) into a blender, pulse, and then pass through a strainer to remove most of the pulp.

Pour the watermelon juice into a large pitcher. Place a generous amount of mint in your hand and slap your hands together to release the oils before adding to the juice. Finally, add the sweet and slightly effervescent muscat. To serve, pour over ice in tall glasses. Stir the mix in the pitcher each time before pouring.

THANK-YOUS

Writing this cookbook was full of discoveries, one of which is how much work goes into writing a cookbook. As amateurs, we had no idea what we were getting ourselves into and now have even more respect for the professionals whose work we have so long admired.

Over the last two years, we ate a lot, cooked a lot, and talked a lot with our family and friends. This book would never have been possible without their support and generosity.

We owe deep thanks to so many:

Lucy Wichmann, recipe assistant, organizer, and cook, was an integral part of this project, without whom we would have been overwhelmed before we started.

Chris Styler, our fearless cookbook mentor, guide, and recipe tester, whose steady hand, patience, and enthusiasm gave us the confidence to keep going.

Eric Wolfinger, our brilliant photographer, and his assistant, **Israel "Izzy" Alemu**, whose beautiful work not only elevated our simple recipes but also captured the vitality of the Carolina coast that underlies all Lowcountry cooking. We learned so much from all of Eric's extraordinary team: **Alma Espinola**, whose keen eye and amazing flair made every table setting look inviting and intimate at the same time. **Alison Attenborough**, our extraordinary food stylist, who understood immediately the high/low balance of our family's cooking, and that a garnish of fresh wildflowers and a sterling silver serving spoon can dress up anything, even boiled peanuts. **Bradley Schaffer**, whose knowledge of Lowcountry cooking was invaluable.

Our wonderfully gifted designer, **Toni Tajima**, whose art and skill made this book even more lovely than we could have hoped.

Lisa Jean Walsh "Muffin," of Who What OUI, our stylist, who kept us looking good and sourced much of the dishware and wardrobe that appear in our photographs.

In addition, these artists and brands helped generously: Billy Reid, Carole Carr Tinkey, Celadon at Home, Estelle Colored Glass, etúHOME, Faherty Brand, Gwynn's of Mount Pleasant, Haand, Juliska, Le Creuset Home, Leigh Magar, M. Dumas & Sons, Nadia Stieglitz, RTW, Sarah Grace Smith with Locals Seafood, and Susan Gregory.

Todd and **Jessica Aaron** and **Wes** and **Betsy Fuller** for their extraordinary generosity.

Special thanks to **Jamie Raab** and **Will Schwalbe** at Celadon Books, who invited us to take this adventure and whose guidance throughout was invaluable. Also at Celadon, our thanks to **Faith Tomlin**, **Christine Mykityshyn**, **Jennifer Jackson**, and **Rachel Chou**. And from the Macmillan production team, **Michelle McMillian**, **Molly Bloom**, and **Emily Walters**. Thanks also to **Dan Strone** from Trident Media Group.

And, as always, we are enormously grateful to our own team: **James Dixon, Carrie Byalick, Amy Cole, Anna Steinmetz,** and **Antonia Xereas**—without whose help, advice, and patience we couldn't do anything.

Finally, deepest thanks go to our beautiful family: our brothers, sisters, nieces, nephews, and parents, who freely shared their recipes and opinions, and our own three children, who have always been our involuntary test kitchen, most honest critics, and biggest cheerleaders.

INDEX

Page numbers in *italics* refer to photographs.

A

Acadia National Park, Maine, 283
All-Purpose Food Processor Pie
    Pastry, 16, 211, 237
    recipe for, 232–33
Almond-Basil Cookies, Cara's,
    249
Almond-Pear Galette, 221, *227*
    recipe for, 226–29
Almonds, Marcona, Stuffed in
    Bacon-Wrapped Dates, 9, *42*
    recipe for, 43
Almonds, Toasted, and
    Cranberries with Wild Rice,
    206, *207*
Alter, Emily Lazar, 128
Another Carrot Cake, *240*,
    241–43, *242–43*
Aperol Spritz (drink), 302, *303*
appetizers. *See* party foods
Arliss, George, 40
Artichoke Dip, Warm, *32*, 33
Arugula Pine Nut Salad, *185*,
    186, *187*
Auggie's Fennel-Bourbon Candied
    Hot Peppers, 24, *26*, 108
    recipe for, 27–28
autolysis process, 216–17

B

Bacon-Wrapped Dates Stuffed
    with Marcona Almonds, 9, *42*
    recipe for, 43
Baked Brie, 280–81, *281*
Balsamic Pearl Onions, 183, *184*

Banana Bread, Paula's, 272–74,
    273
Basil-Almond Cookies, Cara's,
    249
Basil Martini, *300*, 301
bass dishes
    Panfried Spot Tail Bass, 152,
        153
    Sea Bass in White Wine Butter,
        150, *151*
bean dishes
    Chickpea Fries (Panelle), 40,
        52, *54–55*, 102, 196
    Cowboy Caviar, *38*, 39
    Hoppin' John, 198, *200*, 204
    Lentil Soup, 74, *75*
    Sivvy Bean Hummus, 46, 47
beef dishes
    Bill's Beer Brisket, 130–31, *131*
    Christmas Beef Wellington,
        116–17, 116–20, *119–21*, *201*
    Dad's Okra Soup, *76*, 77
    Port Wine Reduction for, *122*,
        123
    Steak au Poivre, *124*, 125–26,
        199
    Stephen's Kindergarten Soup,
        57, *62*, 62–63
beverage strainers, tips for, 301
Big Green Egg grill, 98, 139
Bill's Beer Brisket, 130–31, *131*
biscuit recipes
    Drop Biscuits, *278*, 279
    Patti McGee's Cheese Biscuits,
        12, 12–13

Blueberry Muffins, *268*, 269–71,
    271
Boiled Peanuts, *34*, 34–35
Bolognese Sauce, Lamb, *128*,
    128–29
Bourbon-Brown Sugar Pork
    Belly Sliders, Smoked, with
    Pickled Slaw, 134–36, *135*
Bourbon Chocolate Pecan Pie,
    Mrs. McGee's, 234, *235*
Bourbon-Fennel Candied
    Hot Peppers, Auggie's,
    24, *26*, 108
    recipe for, 27–28
Brando, Marlon, 311
Branton, Mary, 12
bread dishes
    Blueberry Muffins, *268*,
        269–71, *271*
    Buttermilk Cornbread, 208,
        208–9
    Courgette "Madeleines,"
        48–51, *49–50*
    Drop Biscuits, *278*, 279
    Patti McGee's Cheese Biscuits,
        12, 12–13
    Paula's Banana Bread, 272–74,
        273
    Popovers, *282*, 283–85, *284*
    Sourdough Bread, 212–17,
        213–16, *218–19*
breakfast dishes, 260–61
    Blueberry Muffins, *268*,
        269–71, *271*
    Drop Biscuits, *278*, 279

Fig Preserves, 102, 280, *281*
Granola, 275, *276–77*
Hominy Surprise, *290*, 291
Lucy's Espresso Coffee Cake, *262*, 264–66, *265*, *267*
Mom's Shrimp and Hominy, 286–88, *287*
Paula's Banana Bread, 272–74, *273*
Popovers, *282*, 283–85, *284*
Brisket, Bill's Beer, 130–31, *131*
Brownies, Fudgy, 257–58, *259*
Brown Sugar-Bourbon Pork Belly Sliders, Smoked, with Pickled Slaw, 134–36, *135*
Brown Sugar Crumble on Whipped Sweet Potatoes, 188
Brussels Sprouts, Crispy Hot-Honey, *201*, 203
Bunky Cooks Some Soft-Shell Crabs, 172, *173–77*
Bunky Makes Pulled Pork, *138*, 139–41, *140–41*
Bunky Makes Spatchcocked "Yardbird," 96–99, *97–99*
Bunky's "Balled Shrump" (aka Boiled Shrimp), *168*, 169, *170–71*
Burrata and Pistou Provençal with Heirloom Tomato Salad, *190*, 191
Busch, Claus, 34–35, *35*, 36, 204–5
Buttermilk Chicken, Whole Roasted, 110–12, *111*
Buttermilk Cornbread, 208, *208–9*
Buzz Fuzz (drink), 306, *307*
Byalick, Carrie, 33

C
cakes
Carrot, *240*, 241–43, *242–43*
Coffee Espresso, *262*, 264–66, *265*, *267*
Crab, 166, *167*
Calypso Grill, Grand Cayman, 247
Cape Romain Light, South Carolina, 139
Capri Sunset (drink), 311, *311*
Cara's Almond-Basil Cookies, 249
Carlin, Dan, 244
Carrot Cake, Another, *240*, 241–43, *242–43*
Cauliflower Puree, 102, *197*
   recipe for, 196
Cavett, Dick, 311
Caviar, Cowboy, *38*, 39
Cayenne Pepper-Pimento Cheese Spread, 36, *37*
charcoal
   and smoking tips, 136
   sourcing of, 98, 139
Charleston Receipts Cookbook, 2, 150, 182, 257
Charleston, South Carolina, 1, 19–20, 23, 30, 145, 159, 162, 198, 238, 291
   common parlance of, 2, 286
   Spoleto Festival USA in, 15, 95
Cheese Biscuits, Patti McGee's, *12*, 12–13
Cheese Spread, Cayenne Pepper-Pimento, 36, *37*
Cherry Bounce (drink), 308
Chess Pie, *230*, 231
chicken dishes, 82–84, 115
   Bunky Makes Spatchcocked "Yardbird," 96–99, *97–99*
   chicken breast for soups/salads, 61
   Chicken L'Orange, 92–93, *93*

Chicken Thighs with Mustard-Mushroom Sauce, *104*, 104–5
Crunchy Cornflake Chicken with Mango-Cilantro Sauce, 85–86, *87*
Curried Chicken Salad, *94*, 95
Lemon-Chicken-Orzo Soup, *58–59*, 60–61, *61*
Lemon-Pepper Rub for, 100, *100*
Lime-Mezcal Wings, *106*, 108–9
Mango-Cilantro Sauce for, 85–86, *87*
Port Wine Reduction for, *122*, 123
Salt-and-Pepper Wings, *106*, 107, 108
sourcing of chicken for, 96
Spicy Honey-Lemon Chicken Thighs, *88*, 89–90, *91*
Whole Roasted Buttermilk Chicken, 110–12, *111*
Chickpea Fries (Panelle), 40, *52*, *54–55*, 102, 196
   recipe for, 52–53
Chocolate Bourbon Pecan Pie, Mrs. McGee's, 234, *235*
Chowder, Clam, 66–69, *67*
Chowder, Corn, *70*, 71–72
Christmas Beef Wellington, *116–17*, *119–21*, *201*
   recipe for, 116–20
Cilantro-Mango Sauce with Crunchy Cornflake Chicken, 85–86, *87*
Clam Chowder, 66–69, *67*
Claus Boils Some Peanuts, *34*, 34–35
Claus's Collard Greens, *204*, 204–5
Coffee Cake, Lucy's Espresso, *262*, 264–66, *265*, *267*

Colbert, Bill, 130, 150

The Colbert Bump (drink), 308, *308–9*

Colbert, Ed, 125, 159, 253–54, 256

The Colbert Fudge Sibling Saga, *252*, 253–56

Colbert, Jay, 253

Colbert, Jim (father), 20, 145, 150, 224, 295

Colbert, Jim (son), 202, 253

Colbert, John, *109*, 212, *214–16*, *218–19*, *257*, 272, 283

Colbert, Kitty, 40, 125, 159

Colbert, Lorna, 57, 62, 65, 92, 130, 150, 189, 195, 244, 253, 283, 305

Colbert, Lulu, 210, 253, 283, 301

Colbert, Madeleine "Maddie," 48, *81*, 84, 89, *91*, 115

Colbert, Margaret, 295

Colbert, Margo, 210, 253–54, 256

Colbert, Mary, 130, 189, 253, 255

Colbert, Peter, 79, *81*, 83–84, *84*, *109*, *257*, 283

The Colbert Report, 308

Colbert, Susan, 130

Colbert, Tom, 253

Colbert, Vicki, 202

Collard Greens, Claus's, *204*, 204–5

corn dishes

    Buttermilk Cornbread, 208, *208–9*

    Crunchy Cornflake Chicken with Mango-Cilantro Sauce, 85–86, *87*

    Emergency Corn Chowder, *70*, 71–72

    Courgette "Madeleines," 48–51, *49–50*

Covid pandemic, 1–3, 79, 298

Cowboy Caviar, *38*, 39

crab dishes

    Bunky Cooks Some Soft-Shell Crabs, 172, *173–77*

    Crab Cakes, 166, *167*

    Crabmeat Quiche for Cocktail Hour, *14*, 15–16, *17*

    Flounder Stuffed with Deviled Crabmeat, *154*, 155–57

    Hot Crabmeat Dip, 30, *31*

Cranberries and Toasted Almonds with Wild Rice, 206, *207*

Cranston, Bryan, 108

Crisp, Rhubarb (Or Any Fruit, Really), 115, *222–23*, *225* recipe for, 224–25

crisps, blueprint for, 225

Crispy Hot-Honey Brussels Sprouts, *201*, 203

Crunchy Cornflake Chicken with Mango-Cilantro Sauce, 85–86, *87*

La Cuisine Provençale, France, 48

Curried Chicken Salad, *94*, 95

D

Dad's Deviled Eggs, 44, *45*

Dad's Okra Soup, *76*, 77

Dancy, Katie, 39, 60

Dates, Bacon-Wrapped, Stuffed with Marcona Almonds, 9, *42* recipe for, 43

"dead men"/"dead men's fingers," 172

Derrick, Butler, 306

dessert recipes, 220

    All-Purpose Food Processor Pie Pastry, 16, 211, 232–33, 237

    Almond-Pear Galette, 221, 226–29, *227*

    Another Carrot Cake, *240*, 241–43, *242–43*

    Cara's Almond-Basil Cookies, 249

    Chess Pie, *230*, 231

    The Colbert Fudge Sibling Saga, *252,* 253–56

    Fig Tarts for Ina, 221, *236*, 237, 280

    Fudgy Brownies, 257–58, *259*

    Huguenot Torte, 238, *239*

    Key Lime Pie, 250, *251*

    Mrs. McGee's Bourbon Chocolate Pecan Pie, 234, *235*

    Rhubarb (Or Any Fruit, Really) Crisp, 115, *222–23*, 224–25, *225*

    Stephen Candies Some Tangerine Rind, 244–45, *245*, 305

    Sticky Toffee Pudding, *246*, 247–48

Deviled Eggs, Dad's, 44, *45*

Dickerson, Anne, 275

dips/spreads

    Cayenne Pepper-Pimento Cheese Spread, 36, *37*

    Green Goddess Dip, 40, 52

    Hot Crabmeat Dip, 30, *31*

    Sullivan's Island Shrimp Paste, *18*, 19

    Warm Artichoke Dip, *32*, 33

drinks, 294–95, *296–97*

    Aperol Spritz, 302, *303*

    Basil Martini, *300*, 301

    Buzz Fuzz, 306, *307*

    Capri Sunset, 311, *311*

    The Colbert Bump, 308, *308–9*

    Espresso Martini, 298, *299*

    Old Fashioned, *304*, 305

    Les Pieds dans L'eau, *312*, 313, *314–15*

Drop Biscuits, *278*, 279

Duck Breast with Fig-Orange Sauce, 102, *103*

duck fat, 195

Duncan (UPS driver), 249

E

Eggs, Deviled, 44, *45*

Emergency Corn Chowder, *70*, 71–72

Espresso Coffee Cake, Lucy's, *262*, 264–66, *265*, *267*

Espresso Martini, 298, *299*

F

Fennel-Bourbon Candied Hot Peppers, Auggie's, 24, *26*, 108
recipe for, 27–28

Festival dei Due Mondi, Spoleto, Italy, 15

Fig-Orange Sauce with Duck Breast, 102, *103*

Fig Preserves, 102, 280, *281*

Fig Tarts for Ina, 221, *236*, 280
recipe for, 237

"The Fisherman and His Wife" *(Grimms' Fairy Tales)*, 155

Flounder, Fillets, Stuffed, 157

Flounder, Whole, Stuffed with Deviled Crabmeat, *154*, 155–57

Fowler, George, 247

Fries, Chickpea (Panelle), 40, *52*, *54–55*, 102, 196
recipe for, 52–53

Fudge, Colbert Sibling, *252*, 253–56

Fudgy Brownies, 257–58, *259*

G

Galette, Almond-Pear, 221, *227*
recipe for, 226–29

garlic, roasted, tips on, 80

Garten, Ina, 27, 104, 237

Glazed Parsnips, 192, *193*

Goldstein, Sydney, 66

"gospel chicken," 96

Granola, 275, *276–77*

Green Goddess Dip, 40, 52

The Green Goddess (play), 40

grills
smoking meat on, 136
sourcing of, 98–99, 139

Grimms' Fairy Tales (Grimm brothers), 155

grits, 286. *See also* hominy dishes

Gullah Geechee culture, 3, 77

H

Handmade Tomato Soup, *64*, 65

hanger steak, *124*, 125–26

Hardcore History (Carlin), 244

Heirloom Tomato Salad with Pistou Provençal and Burrata, *190*, 191

Hog Island Oyster Company, San Francisco, 66

hominy dishes
Hominy Surprise, *290,* 291
Mom's Hominy and Shrimp, 286–88, *287*

Honeyed, Hot Crispy Brussels Sprouts, *201*, 203

Honey-Lemon Chicken Thighs, Spicy, *88*, 89–90, *91*

Hoppin' John, *200*, 204
recipe for, 198

Hot Crabmeat Dip, 30, *31*

Hot Peppers, Candied, with Fennel-Bourbon, 24, *26*, 108
recipe for, 27–28

Huguenot Torte, 238, *239*

Hummus, Sivvy Bean, *46*, 47

I

the Inca people, 199

J

Jane (French guide), 313

Jane Brody's Good Food Book (Brody), 74, 206

Jim's Spaghetti Squash Casserole, *200*, 202

K

Key Lime Pie, 250, *251*

Kindergarten Soup, Stephen's, 57, *62*
recipe for, 62–63

Kitty's Swordfish with Mustard Cream Sauce, *158*, 159

L

Lamb Bolognese Sauce, *128*, 128–29

The Late Show, 1–3, 27, 182, 249, 298

Lemon-Chicken-Orzo Soup, *58–59*, 60, *61*

Lemon-Honey Chicken Thighs, Spicy, *88*, 89–90, *91*

Lemon-Pepper Rub, 100, *100*

Lentil Soup, 74, *75*

Leo, Maurizio, 214

Lime-Mezcal Wings, *106*, 108–9

Limes, Key Lime Pie with, 250, *251*

Lowcountry culture, 3, 20, 34, 36, 47, 145, 166, 169, 172, 182, 291

Lucy's Espresso Coffee Cake, *262*, 264–66, *265*, *267*

Lulu's Johns Island Tomato Shed Pie, *210*, 210–11

M

"Madeleines," Courgette, 48–51, *49–50*

mandolines, tips on, 199

Mango-Cilantro Sauce with Crunchy Cornflake Chicken, 85–86, *87*

martinis
Basil, *300*, 301
Espresso, 298, *299*

Mary's Potato Salad, 189

McGee, Madeleine (granddaughter), 12, 15, 74, 96, 162, 179, 283

McGee, Madeleine Stoney (grandmother), 208, 231, 279

McGee, Patti, 2, 12–13, 15, 23, 44, 74, 95, 116, 150, 231, 234, 238, 279

McGee, Peter, 12, 44, *45*, 77, 179, 189, 238, 250, 286

meat dishes, 114–15
    Bacon-Wrapped Dates Stuffed with Marcona Almonds, 9, *42*, 43
    Bill's Beer Brisket, 130–31, *131*
    Bunky Makes Pulled Pork, *138*, 139–41, *140–41*
    Christmas Beef Wellington, *116–17*, 116–20, *119–21*, *201*
    Dad's Okra Soup with, *76*, 77
    hanger steak, *124*, 125–26
    Lamb Bolognese Sauce for, *128*, 128–29
    Port Wine Reduction for, *122*, 123
    Smoked Bourbon-Brown Sugar Pork Belly Sliders with Pickled Slaw, 134–36, *135*
    Steak au Poivre, *124*, 125–26, 199
    Stephen's Kindergarten Soup, 57, *62*, 62–63
    Teriyaki Pork Tenderloin, *132*, 133

Menotti, Gian Carlo, 15

Mezcal-Lime Wings, *106*, 108–9

Mom's Shrimp and Hominy, 286–88, *287*

Mrs. McGee's Bourbon Chocolate Pecan Pie, 234, *235*

Muffins, Blueberry, *268*, 269–71, *271*

Mushroom-Mustard Sauce with Chicken Thighs, *104*, 104–5

Mushroom-Parsnip Soup, *78*, 79–80

mushrooms, dried, tips for cooking, 79

Mustard Cream Sauce with Kitty's Swordfish, *158*, 159

Mustard-Mushroom Sauce, *104*, 104–5

N

Nickrenz, Elizabeth, 272

Nickrenz, Scott, 272

Northwestern University, 155

O

Okra Soup, Dad's, *76*, 77

Old Fashioned (drink), *304*, 305

Onions, Pearl, with Balsamic, 183, *184*

Orange-Fig Sauce with Duck Breast, 102, *103*

L'Orange Chicken, 92–93, *93*

Orzo-Lemon-Chicken Soup, *58–59*, 60, *61*

Oyster Pie on the Half-Shell, *160–61*, 162–64, *163–65*

oysters, shucking of, 164, *164*

P

Palace Hotel, San Francisco, 40

Panelle (Chickpea Fries), 40, *52*, *54–55*, 102, 196
    recipe for, 52–53

Panfried Spot Tail Bass, 152, *153*

Paracelsus (alchemist), 295

Parsnip-Mushroom Soup, *78*, 79–80

Parsnips, Glazed, 192, *193*

party foods, 8
    Auggie's Fennel-Bourbon Candied Hot Peppers, 24, *26*, 27–28, 108

Bacon-Wrapped Dates Stuffed with Marcona Almonds, 9, *42*, 43

Cayenne Pepper-Pimento Cheese Spread, 36, *37*

Chickpea Fries (Panelle), 40, *52*, 52–53, *54–55*, 102, 196

Claus Boils Some Peanuts, *34*, 34–35

Courgette "Madeleines," 48–51, *49–50*

Cowboy Caviar, *38*, 39

Crabmeat Quiche for Cocktail Hour, *14*, 15–16, *17*

Dad's Deviled Eggs, 44, *45*

Green Goddess Dip, 40, 52

Hot Crabmeat Dip, 30, *31*

Patti McGee's Cheese Biscuits, *12*, 12–13

Pickled Shrimp, *22*, 23–24, *25*

Sivvy Bean Hummus, *46*, 47

Sullivan's Island Shrimp Paste, *18*, 19

Warm Artichoke Dip, *32*, 33

Patti McGee's Cheese Biscuits, *12*, 12–13

Paul, Aaron, 108

Paula's Banana Bread, 272–74, *273*

Peanuts, Boiled, *34*, 34–35

peanuts, green, sourcing of, 35

Pear-Almond Galette, 221, *227*
    recipe for, 226–29

Pecan Pie with Bourbon Chocolate, Mrs. McGee's, 234, *235*

Pepper and Lemon Rub, 100, *100*

The Perfect Loaf (website), 214

Pickled Shrimp, *22*, 23–24, *25*

Les Pieds dans L'eau (drink), *312*, 313, *314–15*

pie recipes
    All-Purpose Food Processor Pie Pastry, 16, 211, 232–33, 237

Chess Pie, *230*, 231

Key Lime Pie, 250, *251*

Lulu's Johns Island Tomato Shed Pie, *210*, 210–11

Mrs. McGee's Bourbon Chocolate Pecan Pie, 234, *235*

Pimento-Cayenne Pepper Cheese Spread, 36, *37*

Pincus, Sherry, 43, 85

Pine Nut Arugula Salad, *185*, 186, *187*

Pistou Provençal and Burrata with Heirloom Tomato Salad, *190*, 191

Popovers, *282*, 283–85, *284*

pork dishes

    Bacon-Wrapped Dates Stuffed with Marcona Almonds, 9, *42*, 43

    Bunky Makes Pulled Pork, *138*, 139–41, *140–41*

    Christmas Beef Wellington, *116–17*, 116–20, *119–21*, *201*

    Smoked Bourbon-Brown Sugar Pork Belly Sliders with Pickled Slaw, 134–36, *135*

    Teriyaki Pork Tenderloin, *132*, 133

Port Wine Reduction, *122*, 123

potato dishes

    Mary's Potato Salad, 189

    Scalloped Potatoes, 199, *200–201*

    Smashed Potatoes, *194–95*, 195

    Whipped Sweet Potatoes with Brown Sugar Crumble, 188

La Poulete, New York City, 107

poultry dishes, 82–84, 115

    Bunky Makes Spatchcocked "Yardbird," 96–99, *97–99*

    chicken breast for soups/salads, 61

Chicken L'Orange, 92–93, *93*

Chicken Thighs with Mustard-Mushroom Sauce, *104*, 104–5

Crunchy Cornflake Chicken with Mango-Cilantro Sauce, 85–86, *87*

Curried Chicken Salad, *94*, 95

Duck Breast with Fig-Orange Sauce, 102, *103*

Lemon-Chicken-Orzo Soup, *58–59*, 60–61, *61*

Lemon-Pepper Rub for, 100, *100*

Lime-Mezcal Wings, *106*, 108–9

Mango-Cilantro Sauce for, 85–86, *87*

Port Wine Reduction for, *122*, 123

Salt-and-Pepper Wings, *106*, 107, 108

sourcing of birds for, 96

Spicy Honey-Lemon Chicken Thighs, *88*, 89–90, *91*

Whole Roasted Buttermilk Chicken, 110–12, *111*

Pudding, Sticky Toffee, *246*, 247–48

Pulled Pork, Bunky Makes, *138*, 139–41, *140–41*

Q

Quiche, Crabmeat, for Cocktail Hour, *14*, 15–16, *17*

R

"receipts" *vs.* recipes, 2–3

Red Rice, 152, *184–85*

    recipe for, 182

Rhubarb (Or Any Fruit, Really) Crisp, 115, *222–23*, *225*

    recipe for, 224–25

rice recipes

    Red Rice, 152, 182, *184–85*

    Wild Rice with Cranberries and Toasted Almonds, 206, *207*

Robison, Paula, 272

Roemer, Philip, 40

Roloff, Leland, 155

Roman, Alison, 182

Russo, AJ "Auggie," 27–28

S

salad recipes

    Arugula Pine Nut Salad, *185*, 186, *187*

    chicken breast for, 61

    Curried Chicken Salad, *94*, 95

    Heirloom Tomato Salad with Pistou Provençal and Burrata, *190*, 191

    Mary's Potato Salad, 189

    Quick-Pickled Apple-Onion Slaw, 137

Salt-and-Pepper Wings, *106*, 107, 108

The Saltwater Fisherman's Bible (Bauer, Erwin A.), 145

Satow, Jane, 48, 19

sauces

    Fig-Orange, 102, *103*

    Lamb Bolognese, *128*, 128–29

    Mango-Cilantro, 85–86, *87*

    Mustard Cream, *158*, 159

    Mustard-Mushroom, *104*, 104–5

    Pistou Provençal, *190*, 191

    Port Wine Reduction, *122*, 123

    Tartar, 173

    toffee, *246*, 247–48

Scalloped Potatoes, 199, *200–201*

Scoozi, Chicago, 186

Sea Bass in White Wine Butter, 150, *151*

seafood dishes, 144–45, *148–49*

(seafood dishes, *continued*)

Bunky Cooks Some Soft-Shell Crabs, 172, *173–77*

Bunky's "Balled Shrump" (aka Boiled Shrimp), *168,* 169, *170–71*

Clam Chowder, 66–69, *67*

Crab Cakes, 166, *167*

Crabmeat Quiche for Cocktail Hour, *14,* 15–16, *17*

Flounder Stuffed with Deviled Crabmeat, *154,* 155–57

Hot Crabmeat Dip, 30, *31*

Kitty's Swordfish with Mustard Cream Sauce, *158,* 159

Mom's Shrimp and Hominy, 286–88, *287*

Oyster Pie on the Half-Shell, *160–61,* 162–64, *163–65*

Panfried Spot Tail Bass, 152, *153*

Pickled Shrimp, *22,* 23–24, *25*

Port Wine Reduction for, *122,* 123

Sea Bass in White Wine Butter, 150, *151*

Sullivan's Island Shrimp Paste, *18,* 19

Tartar Sauce for, 173

Sedaris, Amy, 152

shrimp dishes

Bunky's "Balled Shrump" (aka Boiled Shrimp), *168,* 169, *170–71*

Mom's Shrimp and Hominy, 286–88, *287*

peeling/deveining process for, 20, 24

Pickled Shrimp, *22,* 23–24, *25*

sourcing of shrimp for, 20, *21,* 169

Sullivan's Island Shrimp Paste, *18,* 19

side dishes. *See* vegetables and side dishes

Simpsons in the Strand, London, 283

Sivvy Bean Hummus, *46,* 47

Slaw, Quick-Pickled Apple-Onion, 137

Sliders, Smoked Bourbon-Brown Sugar Pork Belly, with Pickled Slaw, 134–36, *135*

Smashed Potatoes, *194–95,* 195

Smoked Bourbon-Brown Sugar Pork Belly Sliders with Pickled Slaw, 134–36, *135*

smoking meat, 134, *135, 137*

tips for, 136

Soft-Shell Crabs, 172, *173–77*

soup recipes, 56

chicken breast for, 61

Clam Chowder, 66–69, *67*

Dad's Okra Soup, *76,* 77

Emergency Corn Chowder, *70,* 71–72

Handmade Tomato Soup, *64,* 65

Lemon-Chicken-Orzo Soup, *58–59,* 60, *61*

Lentil Soup, 74, *75*

Mushroom-Parsnip Soup, *78,* 79–80

Stephen's Kindergarten Soup, 57, *62,* 62–63

Sourdough Bread, 212–17, *213–16, 218–19*

Spaghetti Squash Casserole, Jim's, *200,* 202

Spatchcocked "Yardbird," 96–99, *97–99*

Spicy Honey-Lemon Chicken Thighs, *88,* 89–90, *91*

Spoleto Festival USA, Charleston, South Carolina, 15, 95

Steak au Poivre, *124,* 199

recipe for, 125–26

Stephen Candies Some Tangerine Rind, *245,* 305

recipe for, 244–45

Stephen's Kindergarten Soup, 57, *62*

recipe for, 62–63

Stewart, Jon, 298

Sticky Toffee Pudding, *246,* 247–48

Stiles Point Elementary School, James Island, South Carolina, 182

strainers, beverage, tips on, 301

Styler, Chris, 232

Sullivan's Island Shrimp Paste, *18,* 19

Sweet Potatoes, Whipped, with Brown Sugar Crumble, 188

Swordfish with Mustard Cream Sauce, Kitty's, *158,* 159

syrups

caramel, 229

fudge, 254–56

orange, 244–45

tips for, 229, 256

toffee, *246,* 247–48

T

Tangerine Rind, Candied, *245,* 305

recipe for, 244–45

Tartar Sauce, 173

Tartine Bread (Robertson, Chad), 214

Tarts, Fig, for Ina, 221, *236,* 280

recipe for, 237

Teriyaki Pork Tenderloin, *132,* 133

thermometers, tips on, 90

Toffee Pudding, Sticky, *246,* 247–48

tomato dishes

Handmade Tomato Soup, *64,* 65

Heirloom Tomato with Pistou
Provençal and Burrata,
190, 191
Lulu's Johns Island Tomato
Shed Pie, *210*, 210–11
Torte, Huguenot, 238, *239*
truffle honey, tips on, 80

V

vegetables and side dishes,
178–79, *180–81*
Arugula Pine Nut Salad, *185*,
186, *187*
Balsamic Pearl Onions, 183, *184*
Buttermilk Cornbread, 208,
208–9
Cauliflower Puree, 102, 196,
197
Claus's Collard Greens, *204*,
204–5
Crispy Hot-Honey Brussels
Sprouts, *201*, 203

Glazed Parsnips, 192, *193*
Heirloom Tomato Salad
with Pistou Provençal and
Burrata, *190*, 191
Hoppin' John, 198, *200*, 204
Jim's Spaghetti Squash
Casserole, *200*, 202
Lulu's Johns Island Tomato
Shed Pie, *210*, 210–11
Mary's Potato Salad, 189
Red Rice, 152, 182, *184–85*
Scalloped Potatoes, 199,
200–201
Smashed Potatoes, *194–95*,
195
Sourdough Bread, 212–17,
213–16, *218–19*
Whipped Sweet Potatoes with
Brown Sugar Crumble, 188
Wild Rice with Cranberries
and Toasted Almonds,
206, *207*

W

Warm Artichoke Dip, *32*, 33
Washington, Cara, 249
Washington, George, 308
West Africa, 3, 182, 198
Whipped Sweet Potatoes with
Brown Sugar Crumble, 188
Whole Roasted Buttermilk
Chicken, 110–12, *111*
Wichmann, Bunky, 96–99, *99*,
138, 139–41, *140*, *143*, 172,
173
Wichmann, Joe, 203
Wichmann, Lucy, *243*, *264*,
264–66
Wichmann, Theo, 203
Wild Rice with Cranberries and
Toasted Almonds, 206, *207*
Wondrich, Dave, 308

Y

Yorkshire pudding, 283

STEPHEN COLBERT and **EVIE McGEE** both grew up in Charleston, South Carolina, but somehow didn't meet until their midtwenties and decided to get married and have a family.

They are the founders of Spartina Industries, which—aside from producing *The Late Show with Stephen Colbert*, *The Colbert Report*, the critically acclaimed *Derek DelGaudio's In & Of Itself*, *Stephen Colbert Presents Tooning Out The News*, *Hell of a Week with Charlamagne Tha God*, and *Our Cartoon President*—recently penned a three-year first-look deal to develop television and streaming content for CBS Studios. Spartina's most recent project is CBS's newest late-night show, *After Midnight*, starring Taylor Tomlinson, which premiered in January 2024.